I0606306

MYSTERIOUS WORLD

Author: Laura Knowles
Publishing Director: Piers Pickard
Publisher: Rebecca Hunt
Editorial Director: Joe Fullman
Art Director: Andy Mansfield
Print Production: Nigel Longuet

Published in September 2024
by Lonely Planet Global Limited
CRN: 554153
ISBN: 978-1-83758-304-1
1 3 5 7 6 9 10 8 6 4 2

Printed in Malaysia

Stay in Touch
Lonelyplanet.com/contact

Lonely Planet Office:
IRELAND
Digital Depot, Roe Lane (off Thomas St.), Digital Hub, Dublin 8, D08 TCV4, Ireland

Paper in this book is certified against the Forest Stewardship Council™ standards. FSC™ promotes environmentally responsible, socially beneficial and economically viable management of the world's forests.

lonely planet KIDS

MYSTERIOUS WORLD

Laura Knowles

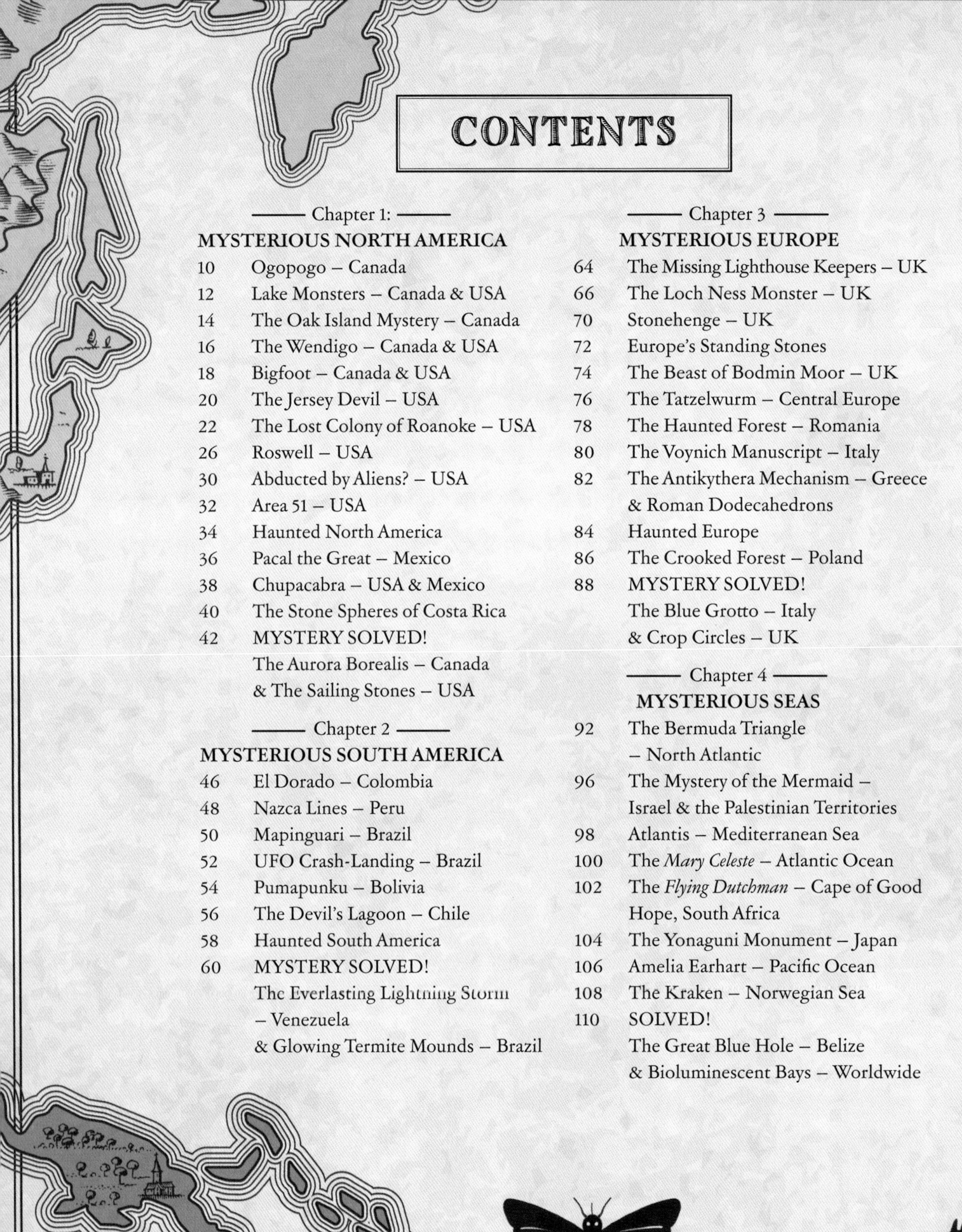

CONTENTS

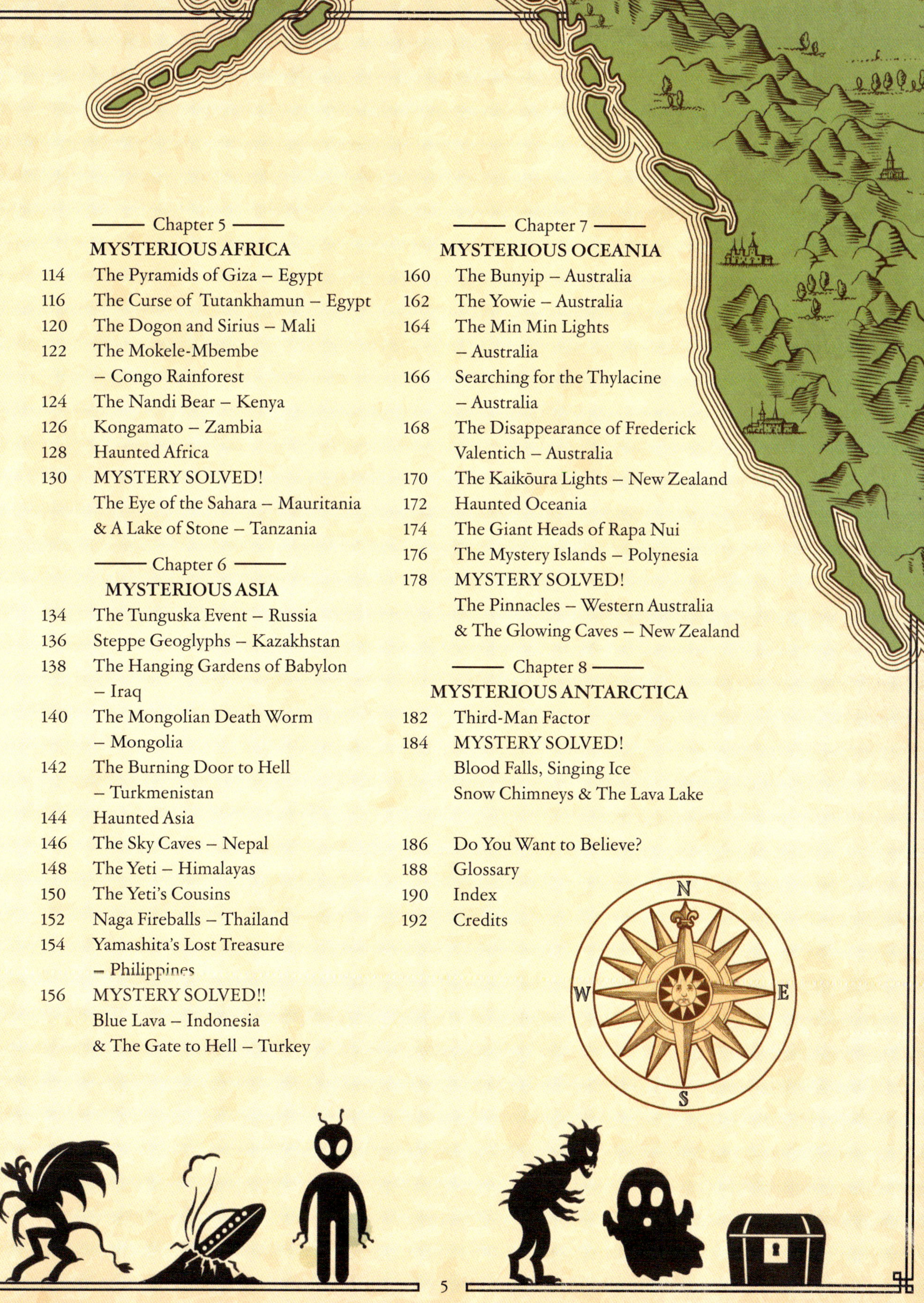

Chapter 5

MYSTERIOUS AFRICA

Chapter 6

MYSTERIOUS ASIA

Chapter 7

MYSTERIOUS OCEANIA

Chapter 8

MYSTERIOUS ANTARCTICA

IT'S A MYSTERIOUS WORLD

If you heard of a legend about a monster that stalked the local woods, would you go looking for it? Or would you hide behind your sofa? And if you heard rumors of treasure buried nearby, would you go digging? For every mystery, there are those who search for answers. From ancient artifacts to UFO sightings, this book delves into just some of the incredible mysteries that can be found on Earth's seven continents and in many seas, including…

ALIENS AND UFOS

Have little green men really visited Earth? And have governments around the world covered up UFO crash-landings to keep us in the dark? Check out Roswell (right and page 26), Area 51 (page 32), and the story of the Brazilian UFO crash-landing (page 52) and judge for yourself if there might be something behind the stories.

LOST TREASURE

Tales of buried gold have tempted many to search fruitlessly for years. Could there be any truth to the rumors of lost riches waiting to be discovered (and the booby traps that protect them)? Find out more by reading the stories behind Oak Island (page 14), El Dorado (above and page 46), and Yamashita's lost treasure (page 154).

CRAZY CRYPTIDS

Every culture has tales of strange creatures that have never been proven to exist. Are there really ape-men hiding out in the forests, such as Bigfoot in North America (below and page 18), the Yeti in Asia (page 148), and the Yowie in Australia (page 162)? And could dinosaur-like monsters have survived deep in lakes around the world, left over from prehistoric times? The people who continue to scour Loch Ness in Scotland every year certainly think so (page 66).

STRANGE STRUCTURES

Ancient civilisations have built structures that still defy explanation, as well as objects that seem far too advanced for their time. How did they achieve such feats? Archaeologists are working feverishly to understand mystifying relics from the past, such as the Nazca Lines (page 48), Stonehenge (right and page 70), and the ancient Antikythera Mechanism, nicknamed the "clockwork computer" (page 82).

GHOSTS

From haunted hotels and theaters, to ghost ships and graveyards, every town seems to have a story about restless spirits that will send a chill down your spine. Each chapter provides a roundup of that continent's most famous hauntings.

UNEXPLAINED DISAPPEARANCES

Throughout the centuries, there are some disappearances that have captured the imagination. What could have happened to the crew of the *Mary Celeste* (left and page 100)? Did Amelia Earhart survive her plane crash (page 106)? Does the Bermuda Triangle really exist (page 92)?

FREAKY PHENOMENA

Some of the biggest mysteries are created by nature, such as the sailing stones of Death Valley (page 43), the blue lava of Indonesia (page 156), or the glowing caves of New Zealand (page 179). In each chapter, you can explore some of Earth's weirdest wonders and discover how what once seemed supernatural has now been explained.

Some mysteries defy reason but live on in the creepy stories we tell each other on dark nights. It can be fun to let ourselves imagine there is more to the world than meets the eye.

SCEPTIC OR BELIEVER?

Mysteries often divide opinion. Some people are certain that ghosts, monsters or aliens exist, while these ideas make others roll on the floor laughing. Some people think that every strange incident has a logical explanation, while others dream up wild conspiracy theories. So which type are you? Does your head tell you there's nothing lurking in the shadows, or does your racing heart feel that monsters just might exist…?

NORTH AMERICA

There is something for every brave traveler who comes to North America in search of mysteries. Adventurers who are eager to delve into the past will find strange structures built by early civilisations in Mexico and Costa Rica, and the lure of buried treasure in Canada. For those looking for aliens and UFOs, the answers might be hidden in the secretive Area 51 in Nevada. But be careful where you go looking: across this continent there are legends of lake monsters, cannibal spirits, the bloodthirsty Chupacabra, and, of course, the infamous Bigfoot.

KEY

1. Aurora Borealis – Canada, p.42
2. Ogopogo – Okanagan Lake, Canada, p.10
3. Tom Thomson's Ghost – Canoe Lake, Canada, p.35
4. Wendigo – Great Lakes region, Canada, p.16
5. Seelkee – Chilliwak, Canada, p.12
6. Memphre – Lake Memphremagog, Canada/USA, p.12
7. Champ – Lake Champlain, USA/Canada, p.13
8. Alien Abduction – New Hampshire, USA, p.30
9. Oak Island Treasure – Nova Scotia, Canada, p.14
10. Igopogo – Lake Simcoe, Canada, p.12
11. Wampus Cat – Appalachian Mountains, USA, p.39
12. Christmas Tree Ship – Lake Michigan, USA, p.35
13. Jersey Devil – Pine Barrens, New Jersey, USA, p.20
14. Mothman – Point Pleasant, West Virginia, USA, p.21
15. Chessie – Chesapeake Bay, USA, p.12
16. Bigfoot – Bluff Creek, California, USA, p.18
17. Old Briney – Great Salt Lake, Utah, USA, p.13
18. Roanoke – North Carolina, USA, p.22
19. Winchester Mystery House – San Jose, California, USA, p.34
20. Roswell – New Mexico, USA, p.26
21. Area 51 – Nevada, USA, p.32
22. Sailing Stones – California, USA, p.43
23. Subway Ghost – Mexico City, Mexico, p.35
24. Tomb of Pacal the Great – Palenque, Mexico, p.36
25. Chupacabra – Puerto Rico, USA, p.38
26. Stone Spheres – Costa Rica, p.40

With only word-of-mouth and blurry photos as evidence, there are still many people who doubt these weird creatures are really out there. So, whatever you do, don't forget to bring your camera.

OGOPOGO

Have you ever swum in a lake or the sea and felt something tickling your toes? You probably thought it was just a fish or a bit of vegetation. But have you ever wondered if there might be weird creatures hiding beneath the surface, yet to be discovered? In Okanagan Lake in British Columbia, Canada, there have long been stories of a mysterious beast lurking in the depths. Named Ogopogo, it doesn't sound like the kind of creature you'd want to swim too close to...

The newly named Ogopogo became so famous it was used in advertisements, such as this one for apples from the 1920s.

FIRST NAMES

The Syilx First Nations people, who lived near the lake for thousands of years before European settlers arrived in Canada, called the creature N'ha-a-itk, which means "sacred spirit of the lake," and described it as having the head of a horse and deer's antlers.

MISUNDERSTANDINGS

When European settlers arrived, stories began to spread about a monstrous creature. It was said that the serpent demon would whip up a storm with its tail and drown anyone who traveled across the lake without first sacrificing an animal to it. However, it has been claimed that these tales were based on a European misunderstanding, and that the Indigenous peoples regarded N'ha-a-itk as a peaceful protector of the area.

NEW NAME

The modern name Ogopogo comes from a catchy 1920s' song about a strange creature called an Ogo-Pogo. The lyrics went "His mother was an earwig; His father was a whale; A little bit of head; And hardly any tail; And Ogopogo was his name." Even though the song wasn't about the Canadian lake creature, the funny name stuck.

EVIDENCE AND EXPLANATIONS

CAUGHT ON VIDEO?

There have been countless reported sightings of Ogopogo over the centuries. These days, everyone can take photos and videos on their phones, so more evidence is being gathered that there really might be something lurking in the lake. In 2019, a local man took a video of what he thinks is Ogopogo. It looked like a long series of humps moving quickly along the surface of the water.

Could the humps have belonged to a giant lake creature?

Could the monster really be just a group of swimming beavers, like these?

WAVE FOR THE CAMERA

Some people claim that the monster is just a case of mistaken identity, and the sightings are of a normal animal (or animals) swimming across the lake, such as a beaver, an otter, or a school of fish. A scientist looking at the 2019 video evidence thinks that it shows an unusual kind of wave that forms when water layers of different temperatures pass each other.

A MONSTER MASCOT

Whatever the truth, the legend of Ogopogo lives on. In fact, the local town even has an Ogopogo statue (below) and sells lake monster souvenirs.

A MONSTER MILLIONAIRE

There are some who won't rest until they have tracked down the monster once and for all. In the 1980s, the local tourism association offered a $1 million reward for proof that the mysterious lake monster existed. Could you be the one to finally capture this cryptid and claim the reward?

LAKE MONSTERS

Ogopogo (page 10) shouldn't feel lonely. Across the world, there have been many claims of lake monster sightings, and North America has its fair share. Here are a few of the legendary creatures that keep rearing their serpentine heads in this part of the world.

MEMPHRE

This elusive monster is said to live in Lake Memphremagog, which lies on the border between Quebec in Canada and Vermont in the United States. Stories of a watery beast may have their origin in a Viking rock carving of a serpent on a nearby mountain. Over the years, many people have claimed to have seen the monster, which has even been featured on a collectable coin.

IGOPOGO

Igopogo gets its name from its more famous cousin, Ogopogo. It has also been nicknamed Beaverton Bessie and Kempenfelt Kelly after locations around Lake Simcoe in Ontario, Canada, where the monster is said to live. It is often described as looking like a serpent, and similar to Ogopogo or the Loch Ness Monster, though those who don't believe it exists have suggested that the sightings may be of otters or beavers swimming in the distance.

CHESSIE

Chessie (the American Nessie!) is said to live in Chesapeake Bay, Maryland. As the bay connects to the Atlantic Ocean, this technically makes Chessie a sea monster, though it does appear to stick close to the shore. People can't agree on when Chessie was first spotted, but it seems to have been in the 1930s or 1940s. Sceptics argue that the sightings could be mistaken identity, and that Chessie is nothing more than a manatee that has strayed from its usual habitat.

SEELKEE

Said to live in the swamps of Chilliwack in British Columbia, Canada, the Seelkee is described as looking similar to the Ogopogo, but with two heads and red markings on its dark skin. Carvings of the legendary Seelkee decorated the longhouses of Indigenous peoples in the area.

Could a manatee, such as this one, really be mistaken for a terrifying lake monster?

ADMIT ONE

Lake monsters are considered so terrifying, they have even been the subject of horror movies. This is a poster from a 1977 film about a deadly plesiosaur in Crater Lake, California.

ADMIT ONE

THE CRATER LAKE MONSTER

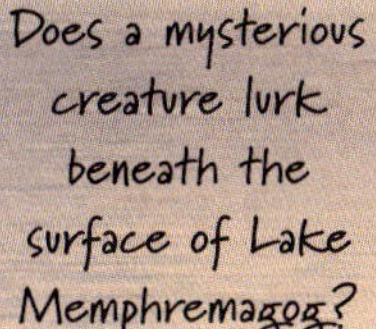

Does a mysterious creature lurk beneath the surface of Lake Memphremagog?

CHAMP

Named after Lake Champlain, sandwiched between New York and Vermont, this lake monster was first sighted in 1609. The most famous photo of what is claimed to be Champ was taken by Sandra Mansi in 1977. It looks like a prehistoric beast with a long neck… but others claim it could just be a floating tree stump.

OLD BRINEY

Also known as the North Shore Monster, this unusual creature is said to lurk in the Great Salt Lake in Utah. One sighting in 1877 described the monster as having a body like a crocodile and a head like a horse. Other stories tell of a creature that looks like the tiny brine shrimp that live in the lake, but the size of a big dog, or larger. If the tales are true, could it be some sort of prehistoric sea creature that has survived in the salty lake waters?

THE OAK ISLAND MYSTERY

For 200 years, treasure hunters have been searching Oak Island, a small island in Nova Scotia, Canada. They are trying to find gold believed to have been buried by the notorious pirate from the "Golden Age of Piracy," Captain Kidd.

An aerial view of Oak Island, where many people believe Captain Kidd buried his treasure

Who was Captain Kidd?

Born: 1645, Scotland

Died: 1701, Execution Dock, London, England

Captain William Kidd was a pirate who was hanged for his crimes. Some of his treasure was dug up on Gardiners Island, off the coast of New York. According to legend, one of his crew claimed that treasure worth $4 million had also been buried on Oak Island.

DIGGING DEEPER AND DEEPER

- The first attempt to retrieve the gold was made in 1795. A shaft was dug down into soil that seemed loosely packed, as if someone had already dug there before. However, no treasure was recovered.
- Many more attempts were made to find the treasure in the 1800s. Though treasure-hunters dug down to 110 ft. (33 m), the holes kept flooding with seawater, which some people claim was a booby trap laid to stop looters reaching the treasure.
- A shaft was dug down to 135 ft. (41 m) in 1965, but still nothing was found.
- In 1971, a shaft was dug all the way to solid rock, 235 ft. (72 m) down, but it later collapsed. Before it did, a camera was sent down. Some claimed that these photos showed human remains, tools, and chests, but others said that it was impossible to make out what was in the murky images. The shaft was re-dug in 2016, but nothing was found.

THE CURSE

It's been said that the treasure will only be found once seven people have died trying to find it. So far, six men are believed to have died. They are listed on this memorial stone on the island.

A STONE MARKS THE SPOT?

It was reported that a strange stone had been found the second time the shaft was dug, in 1802. The stone was about 2 ft. (60 cm), with symbols carved onto it. Since then, people inspecting the stone have argued about whether the marks, now worn away, were truly symbols or just natural markings. It's even been claimed that the markings were translated as "Forty feet below, four million dollars are buried," but it's not clear how someone could have deciphered the message.

CONFUSING COCONUTS

Puzzlingly, large amounts of coconut fibers have been found on Oak Island, even though coconuts don't grow there. Could the fibers have been transported from the Caribbean by pirates or other sailors, and used as packing material or ropes? Carbon dating has shown that some of the fibers are more than 700 years old.

TREASURE LEGENDS

There have been many rumors of what kind of treasure might be hidden on Oak Island. As well as Captain Kidd's gold, it's also been claimed that the island might hold secret manuscripts, the missing French crown jewels, or even the Holy Grail.

WHAT ELSE COULD IT BE?

It may be that there isn't any buried treasure on Oak Island. The first people to dig the shaft thought they were digging out a pit that had been filled in to hide the treasure. But others have argued that it may just have been a natural sinkhole that had filled up with loose earth over the years. But there are still plenty who believe the treasure is down there, tantalizingly out of reach—all they need to do to get it is dig down a little farther...

THE WENDIGO

Imagine you are trekking through the northern wilderness. Winter's bitter wind bites at your cheeks, and the deep snowdrifts pull at your legs. Hungry, you just want to make it back to your cabin before the long night draws in. You hear a rustling from the trees, a long shadow flits past you. Is it a deer? Another hiker? ... Or could it be the dreaded Wendigo?

WHAT IS THE WENDIGO?

In the myths of the Algonquian-speaking peoples of North America, the Wendigo is a cannibal spirit. It is sometimes described as a grotesque beast that eats humans, stalking them through the cold winter landscape. In other tales, it is an evil spirit that possesses humans, turning them into cannibals who prey on their own friends and neighbors.

The earliest descriptions of the Wendigo show it without antlers, while most modern depictions have long antlers.

BEWARE THE CANNIBAL SPIRIT

The fearsome Wendigo is said to have superhuman strength, speed, and senses, making it a frightening predator able to catch its human prey with ease. People living in towns and cities should be able to let their guard down, though. Wendigos haunt the snowy forests and wilderness of Canada and the northern United States and aren't known to stray into densely populated areas.

MANY NAMES

The Wendigo goes by more than 30 names beginning with *W*, including Windigo, Windigoo, Wetiko, and Widjigo.

WHAT DOES IT LOOK LIKE?

According to some legends, the Wendigo is skeleton thin, with sickly gray skin and sunken eyes. Its lips are chewed and blood-stained. It's said to be always hungry, thinking of nothing but devouring its next meal. Other descriptions say the Wendigo is a giant, towering more than twice as high as a regular man. The more it eats, the larger it grows, meaning it's never full. It is sometimes described as having a mouth full of sharp teeth and eyes that glow in the dark.

It is said that people can detect a Wendigo by its horrible stench, thought to smell like rotting flesh.

In some Native American folklore, a person turns into a Wendigo if they eat another human to survive.

The Wendigo is said to wander the frozen wastes of the Great Lake region and eastern Canada.

DEFEATING A WENDIGO

It's believed that the only way to stop a Wendigo is to cut out its heart and destroy it in a fire. It has also been said that a shaman (holy person) can defeat a Wendigo using a silver bullet or dagger.

IS THE WENDIGO REAL?

Many people don't believe the Wendigo is a real monster. Instead, they say that it's an invented creature that represents the dangers of winter, hunger, greed, and of acting selfishly. Fear of the cannibal monster encourages people to stick together and share resources. Or maybe that's what it wants you to think...

BIGFOOT

A large, hairy creature is said to roam the mountain wildernesses of northwestern USA and western Canada. Perhaps the most notorious figure in cryptozoology, it is, of course, the world-famous Bigfoot. Described as being part-ape, part-human, this solitary character has so far escaped capture. Though many doubt the creature exists, there are still plenty of believers on the hunt for evidence...

This US statue of Bigfoot is a giant, at 28 ft. (8.5 m) tall.

HOW TALL?

It's been claimed that Bigfoot is a big, powerful creature capable of throwing boulders and bashing down trees. However, eyewitnesses can't seem to agree on its height. Some accounts say the beast is only around 6 ft. (2 m) tall, while others have claimed it is as much as 15 ft. (4.5 m). Perhaps the confusion comes from only seeing the strange animal from a distance.

WHAT'S THE EVIDENCE?

Though some photos, films, and eye-witness accounts have been put forward over the years to prove Bigfoot exists, no individuals have been captured, alive or dead. The most famous sighting of Bigfoot was caught on camera by Roger Patterson at Bluff Creek in California in 1967 (left). Is this a genuine image of a hairy cryptid, or a man in an ape suit?

HAIR

Samples of hair have been collected, which Bigfoot-believers say have come from the beast itself. However, scientists have tested the DNA of many of the samples and have found that most of them are actually bear fur, and the rest are from other known animals.

FOOTPRINTS

The largest footprints said to come from Bigfoot are a whopping 23 in. (60 cm) long and 8 inches (20 cm) wide, though others are much smaller. Some of these prints have even been preserved as plaster casts (right). However, it can't be proven that they were really made by Bigfoot, and some people have been accused of making fake footprints.

SKUNK APE

A southern cousin of Bigfoot is said to dwell in the forests and swamps of Florida (below). Known as the Skunk Ape, because of its disgusting, skunk-like smell, the beast is said to be covered in reddish-brown hair, but smaller than Bigfoot. Though reported sightings date back to the early 19th century, no solid evidence has been found to convince sceptics that this creature exists.

WHAT COULD IT BE?

A HOAX?

With Bigfoot escaping capture despite its decades of fame, there are many who say that the film footage and footprints are nothing but a hoax. A few people have even admitted carving big wooden feet in order to make fake footprints. Some hoaxers have dressed up in a hairy costume, pretending to be the fabled creature.

MISTAKEN IDENTITY?

It has been suggested that some of the Bigfoot sightings are actually bears, which are known to sometimes walk on their hind legs. Other sightings might be of escaped gorillas or chimpanzees, or simply humans wearing animal pelts.

JUST REALLY GOOD AT HIDING?

Could there be simple explanations for all the many sightings? Is it worth considering that perhaps the creature is now so wary of the attention, it has become an expert at hiding whenever it sees people coming close?

THE JERSEY DEVIL

Since the 1800s, there have been tales of a fearsome winged "demon" lurking in the forests of the Pine Barrens, in New Jersey and Philadelphia, and killing farm animals. Then, in a single week in January 1909, the beast and its tracks were supposedly seen by many hundreds of people. The local communities became so scared that some schools were shut down and people stayed home from work. Despite hunters searching for the terrifying creature, no evidence was found.

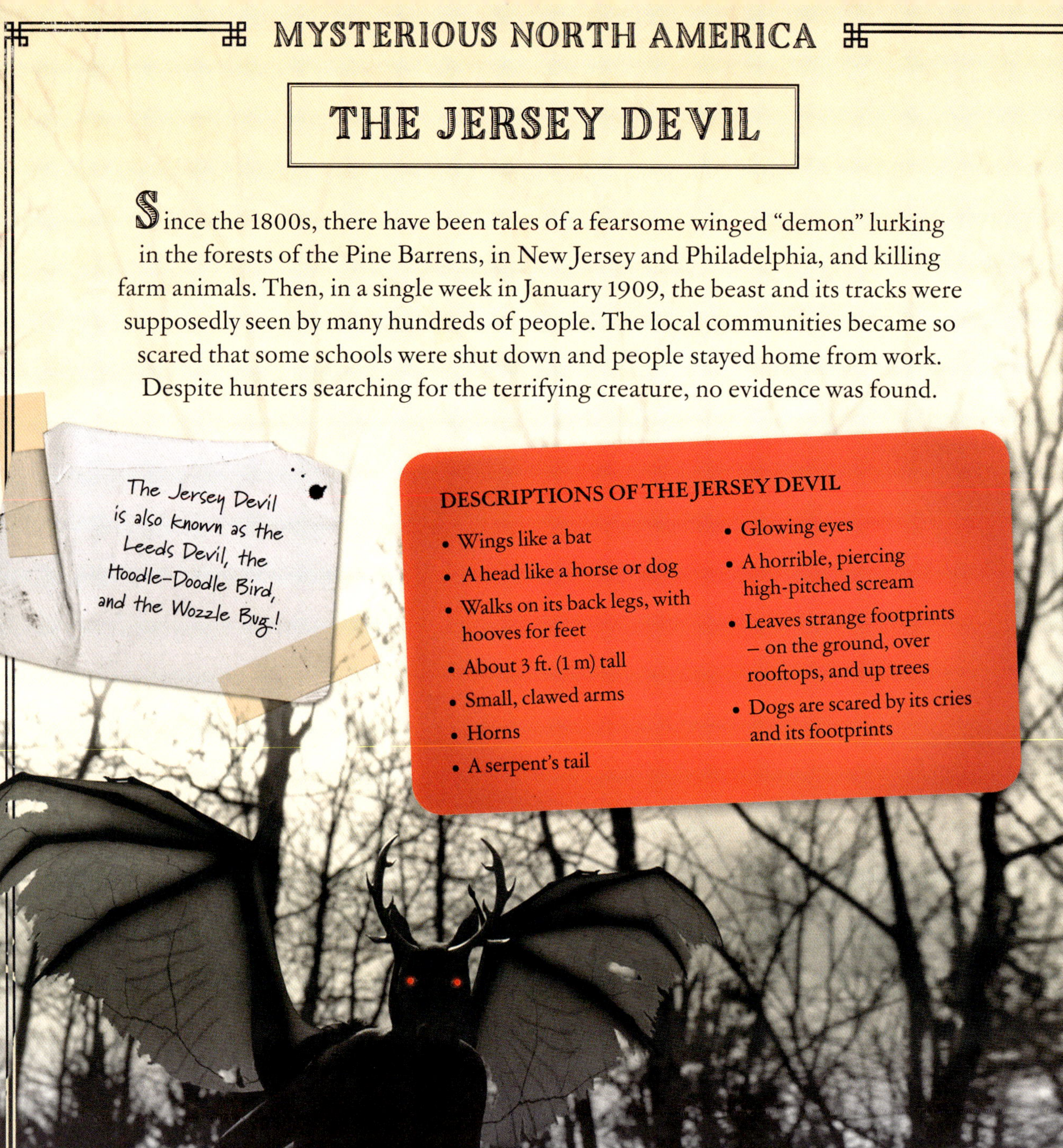

The Jersey Devil is also known as the Leeds Devil, the Hoodle-Doodle Bird, and the Wozzle Bug!

DESCRIPTIONS OF THE JERSEY DEVIL

- Wings like a bat
- A head like a horse or dog
- Walks on its back legs, with hooves for feet
- About 3 ft. (1 m) tall
- Small, clawed arms
- Horns
- A serpent's tail
- Glowing eyes
- A horrible, piercing high-pitched scream
- Leaves strange footprints – on the ground, over rooftops, and up trees
- Dogs are scared by its cries and its footprints

BIRTH OF A DEVIL

There are many versions of the legend about how the Jersey Devil came to exist. One story is that the monster was the child of a woman—sometimes called Mother Leeds—who lived in Leeds Point, New Jersey, in 1735. Having already had 12 children, she supposedly said that if she ever became pregnant again, the child would be a devil. When the baby was born, it had wings and flew out of the house and into the wild.

WHAT COULD IT BE?

AN ANCIENT SPIRIT?

The Indigenous Lenape people of the region told stories of a spirit called M'Sing, said to look similar to a deer, but with leathery wings. Is this a coincidence, or could the legend of the Jersey Devil be inspired by tales of M'Sing?

A BIG BIRD?

Some people claim the "devil" could simply be a large bird such as a crane, but this doesn't match most of the descriptions. A crane wouldn't have been able to kill farm animals. Perhaps wolves or coyotes were responsible for the animal deaths, and a glimpse of a large bird made people think they had seen the famous winged demon.

A PREHISTORIC BEAST?

Others suggest that the monster may be some sort of pterosaur that survived prehistoric times. But if that's the case, there would have to be a lot more of the creatures. How come nobody has found more evidence of them? How could they have survived when all other flying reptiles went extinct millions of years ago?

WILD IMAGINATIONS?

Perhaps there was never a wild creature on the loose. Maybe it was people's imaginations running wild instead. When scary stories are shared, it can make people nervous, more ready to jump to conclusions, and trick them into thinking they have seen or heard the same thing.

THE MOTHMAN

Giant birds—specifically sandhill cranes—have also been put forward as a possible explanation for sightings of another mystery creature seen in Point Pleasant, West Virginia, in 1967: the Mothman. Said to resemble a giant moth with glowing eyes, it was reportedly seen numerous times between November 15 and December 15, when a suspension bridge in Point Pleasant collapsed. Some believe the sightings and the disaster were connected. These events were explored in the 1970s book and 2002 film, *The Mothman Prophecies*.

THE LOST COLONY OF ROANOKE

Today, more than 340 million people live in the United States, but back in 1587, it was a very different land. There were several million Native Americans, whose ancestors had lived on the land for thousands of years, but Europeans were only just starting to build settlements there. The fate of one early group of settlers—including the first English baby born in North America—is a mystery that remains unsolved to this day.

THE FIRST COLONIES

In 1585, the first English colony was established on Roanoke Island, on what is now the east coast of the United States. The 108 colonists built cabins and a protective fort, but they didn't get on well with the local Native Americans, and soon ran out of food. After just 11 months, they abandoned the settlement and returned to England. Not long after, another ship arrived at the abandoned Roanoke Colony. It left some men there, along with enough supplies for two years.

The first Roanoke fort of 1585, as imagined by an artist in the 1960s

Roanoke as illustrated by John White

TRYING AGAIN

England hadn't given up hope of establishing a permanent colony in America. In July 1587, a new group of settlers landed on Roanoke Island, led by the explorer and artist John White. There were 90 men, 17 women, and 11 children. When they arrived, they found the old colony deserted. The handful of men who had arrived the year before had disappeared without a trace. Would this be an ominous sign of things to come?

FIRST BABY

John White's daughter, Eleanor, was one of the Roanoke settlers. On August 18, less than a month after they had arrived, Eleanor had a baby, which was named Virginia Dare. Her name was to go down in history as the first English child born in the "New World" of the Americas. Sadly, she vanished along with the other settlers.

A 19th-century depiction of the baptism of Virginia Dare

A DELAYED RETURN

Just a month after the group arrived, John White returned to England. He planned to get more supplies, which the colony desperately needed. Unfortunately, his return trip was delayed because of a war between England and Spain, and so he couldn't reach Roanoke Island until three years later, in 1590. When he finally got there, he discovered to his horror that the colony was gone.

In this 19th-century image, John White is shown next to what he thinks is a message from the missing colonists.

A CARVED CLUE?

John White discovered the word "Croatoan" carved into a post, and "Cro" carved into a tree. He thought that this might be a message left for him by the settlers to say they had moved to live with the friendly Croatoan tribe on nearby Croatoan Island. However, the ship White had sailed on was damaged. It had lost two of its three anchors, and the captain was unwilling to lose the final one exploring Croatoan Island. So White was forced to sail back to England. He was still hopeful that the colony had simply relocated.

Around 17 years later, when settlers from Jamestown Colony in Virginia searched for the missing people, they found no trace of the colony on Roanoke or Croatoan Islands. Perhaps they never made it to Croatoan after all? Turn the page to find out what might have happened…

WHAT HAPPENED TO THE COLONISTS?

KILLED?

Many think it is likely that the settlers were killed by Native Americans. After all, the colonists had arrived from far away and were trying to hunt and farm on land the native peoples already lived on. Relations between the newcomers and the original peoples were often hostile. However, there is no evidence that the colony met a brutal end on Roanoke Island. If they were killed, perhaps it was after they had moved to another place.

BAD LUCK?

Scientists have figured out that the years when the settlers were trying to build the Roanoke Colony were unusually dry, which would have made farming difficult. On top of that, many of the settlers had little experience of farming and hunting. Unless they were able to make friends and trade goods with a local tribe, they may not have survived. Could it be that many of the colony died of illness and hunger? But if so, wouldn't they have left graves and messages for others to find?

THE DARE STONES

In 1937, long after the Roanoke Colony had vanished, a mysterious stone was discovered in a swamp. It was carved with a message supposedly written by Eleanor Dare, daughter of John White. It said that her husband and child had died in 1591 and that more than half the settlers had died of sickness or been killed by local tribes. Another 47 stones were later found, but many people think these are fake. However, it's not clear whether the original stone is real or a fake—experts are still examining it to try to figure that out.

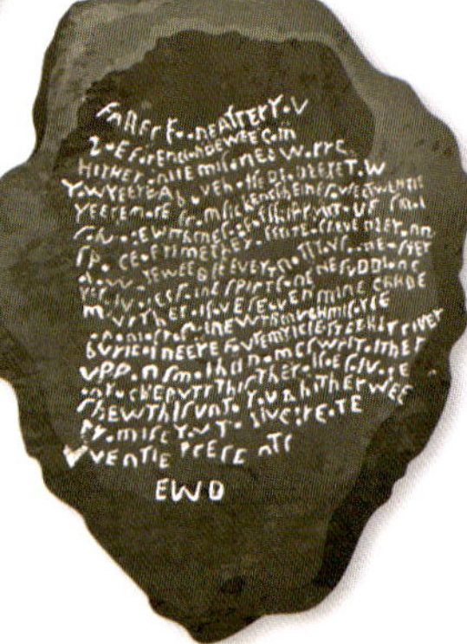

The stones are housed in Brenau University, Georgia.

Does the island's modern lighthouse stand above the ruins?

VANISHED TOWN

It wasn't just the settlers who couldn't be found. The colony's town has also mysteriously disappeared. Archaeologists have uncovered the remains of a workshop, but little else. Some geologists think the ruins may have been washed away by rising sea levels, but archaeologists disagree.

LIVING WITH THE LOCALS?

It has been suggested that the colony may have gone to live with a local tribe, and that later settlers simply never found them. Since it would have been very challenging to start a new life in a strange new land, this might have been the settlers' best chance for survival. If the Roanoke settlers did join up with the Croatoans, their story may still not have a happy ending. It is thought the Croatoan tribe was later wiped out by smallpox, a deadly disease that was brought to the Americas by later European settlers.

Could the settlers have ended up living in a Native American village, such as Pomeiooc, shown here in a watercolor image by John White?

This is a modern replica of the ship that brought the settlers.

GONE BUT NOT FORGOTTEN

Though few traces of the lost colony remain, its founding and disappearance are still remembered today. At the 27-acre Roanoke Island Festival Park, close to the original settlement, visitors can learn what life was like for both the settlers and the Native Americans already living here at the end of the 16th century.

ROSWELL

In 1947, during a lightning storm on a ranch near the city of Roswell in New Mexico, a mysterious flying object crashed to Earth, scattering strange wreckage across the ground. What followed would spark one of the biggest conspiracy theories in history, with many people claiming the US government had covered up an alien crash landing.

WHAT HAPPENED?

After the storm, a farmer called Mac Brazel found unusual debris on his ranch outside Roswell. It was made of various strange metallic and rubber-like objects. The material was small and light enough to fit inside a car trunk, so he took it to the local sheriff, who gave it to a nearby US military air base to investigate.

EYEWITNESS DESCRIPTIONS

"The debris looked like pieces of a large balloon which had burst ... Most of it was a kind of double-sided material, foil-like on one side and rubber-like on the other. Both sides were grayish silver in color ... Sticks, like kite sticks, were attached to some of the pieces with a whitish tape."

– Bessie Brazel, the rancher's daughter

"Brazel ... showed my husband and me a piece of material ... brown in color, similar to plastic ... Mac said the other material on the property looked like aluminum foil. It was very flexible and wouldn't crush or burn."

– Loretta Proctor, the rancher's neighbor

Roswell Daily

Roswell, New Mexico, Tuesday, July 8, 1947

1888

RAAF Ca

On Ranch

Claims Army Is Stacking Courts Martial

Indiana Senator Lays Protest Before Patterson

Washington, July 8 (AP)—Senator Jenner (R-Ind.) contended today that "the high command in the European theatre is stacking courts against defendants in court martial."

In a letter to Secretary of War Patterson demanding a full investigation of army military trial procedure, Jenner offered what he said was documentary proof that:

1. "Prisoners are not being permitted to employ either civilian or military counsel of their own choice in the preparation and presentation of their defense."

2. "Every effort is being made to prevent attorneys who were connected with the infamous Lichfield

House Passes Tax Slash by Large Margin

Defeat Amendment By Demos to Remove Many from Rolls

Washington, July 8 (AP) — The house passed today the Republican-backed bill to cut income taxes by $4,000,000,000 annually for 49,000,000 taxpayers, beginning Jan. 1.

It goes to the senate where approval also is forecast.

Security Coun Paves Way to On Arms Red

EXPLANATION... OR COVER-UP?

To begin with, the US Air Force announced that the wreckage was part of a "flying disc." They then changed this statement, claiming instead that it was a weather balloon. Brazel, the rancher who found the mysterious wreckage, told a local paper that he didn't think it came from a weather balloon.

THE FLYING SAUCER CRAZE

Just a month before the "Roswell Incident," a US pilot named Kenneth Arnold had reported seeing nine strange, shiny objects flying in the sky at an incredible speed. This was the first report of what we now think of as "UFOs" (unidentified flying objects), and it sparked interest across America. Suddenly, many other people were claiming to have spotted UFOs too. Did this make people more likely to jump to the conclusion that the wreckage at Roswell was an alien UFO… or were there actually lots of extraterrestrials visiting Earth?

An artistic impression of what some people think happened at Roswell.

Record

RECORD PHONES
Business Office 2288
News Department
2287

5¢ PER COPY

res Flying Saucer
Roswell Region

o Details of
lying Disk
Are Revealed

Roswell Hardware
Man and Wife
Report Disk Seen

The intelligence office of the 509th
Bombardment group at Roswell
Army Air Field announced at noon
today, that the field has come into
possession of a flying saucer.
According to information released
by the department, over authority of
Maj. J.A. Marcel, intelligence officer,
the disk was recovered on a ranch in
the Roswell vicinity, after an uniden-
…had notified Sheriff

Ex-King Carol Weds Mme. Lupescu

ALIEN WRECKAGE

Intelligence officer Jesse Marcel (below) was one of the people from the military air base who visited the ranch to investigate the wreckage. Over 30 years later, Marcel claimed that the weather balloon was a cover story. He said that the real wreckage had been swapped with weather balloon debris, and that it had been an alien spacecraft after all. This astounding claim raises many questions. Could this have been true? Might Jesse Marcel have misremembered, or could he have made it all up to get attention? Why did he decide to tell this story so many years later? Turn the page to examine the evidence…

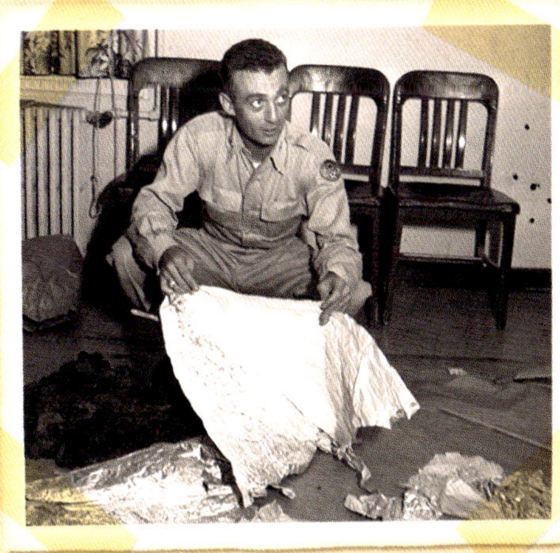

SPY IN THE SKY

In 1994, the US Air Force revealed that the Roswell wreckage wasn't a weather balloon as they had previously stated. Now, they claimed it was in fact a spy balloon, such as the ones on the left, which had been used in a top-secret operation called Project MOGUL. Its purpose had been to detect nuclear bomb tests carried out by the Soviet Union, which was the USA's enemy at the time. However, this revelation didn't satisfy everyone. In the nearly 50 years since the mysterious event at Roswell, many people had become sure that the US government was covering up an alien crash landing.

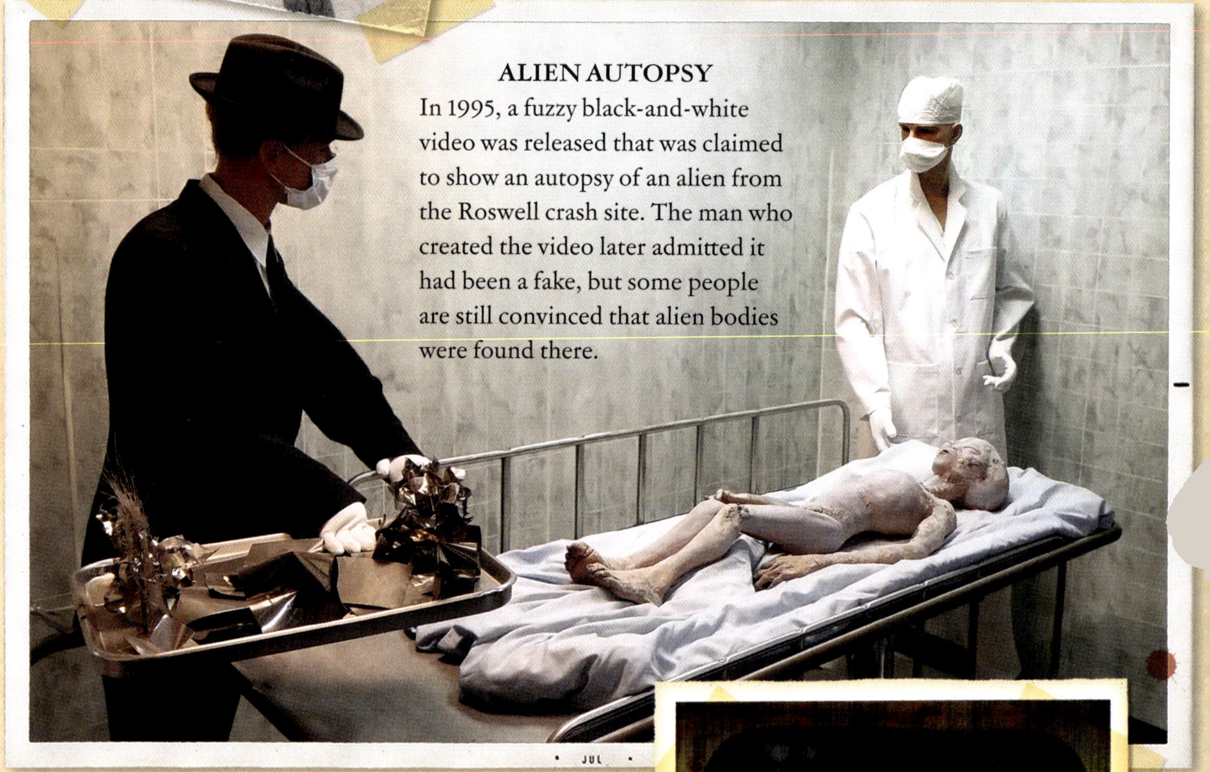

ALIEN AUTOPSY

In 1995, a fuzzy black-and-white video was released that was claimed to show an autopsy of an alien from the Roswell crash site. The man who created the video later admitted it had been a fake, but some people are still convinced that alien bodies were found there.

A model of the autopsy video at Roswell's UFO Museum

STRANGE RUMORS

The idea that aliens were found at the Roswell crash site has been fueled by rumors from the military base where the wreckage was taken. A soldier called John Tilley arrived at the base six months after the incident and said he heard talk that "something" had escaped and was peering through windows, scaring people. Could there be truth to these rumors, or were people just having fun with a scary story?

CRASH-TEST DUMMIES

In 1997, the US government wrote a report about the Roswell Incident to try to stop the conspiracy theories once and for all. In it, they suggested that people who thought aliens had been found at the site might have been misremembering seeing fallen parachute test dummies (right), or even an injured parachutist who crashed nearby a few years later. But many people aren't convinced.

TOP SECRET

TOP SECRET

There is a conspiracy theory that UFO wreckage and alien bodies found at Roswell were taken to a top-secret location called Area 51 to be studied and reverse engineered—the process of taking apart a machine or product to figure out how it was made, so you can make your own version. Turn to page 32 to find out more about Area 51.

ALIEN CITY

Whether you believe it was an alien crash landing, an air force conspiracy or all just a lot of fuss about nothing, the events of 1947 have put the city of Roswell on the map. Today, the word "Roswell" instantly conjures up images of little gray men and flying saucers. The city has its own UFO museum and hosts a UFO festival every year.

WELCOME TO
ROSWELL

Roswell's street signs play up its alien connections.

WHAT DO YOU THINK?

Conspiracy theories have been fueled by the US government changing its story several times. However, there isn't any physical evidence of a UFO or aliens at Roswell, and a lot of the claims have come from people remembering events many years later. What do you think? Could something as big as aliens crashing to Earth have been covered up for so long?

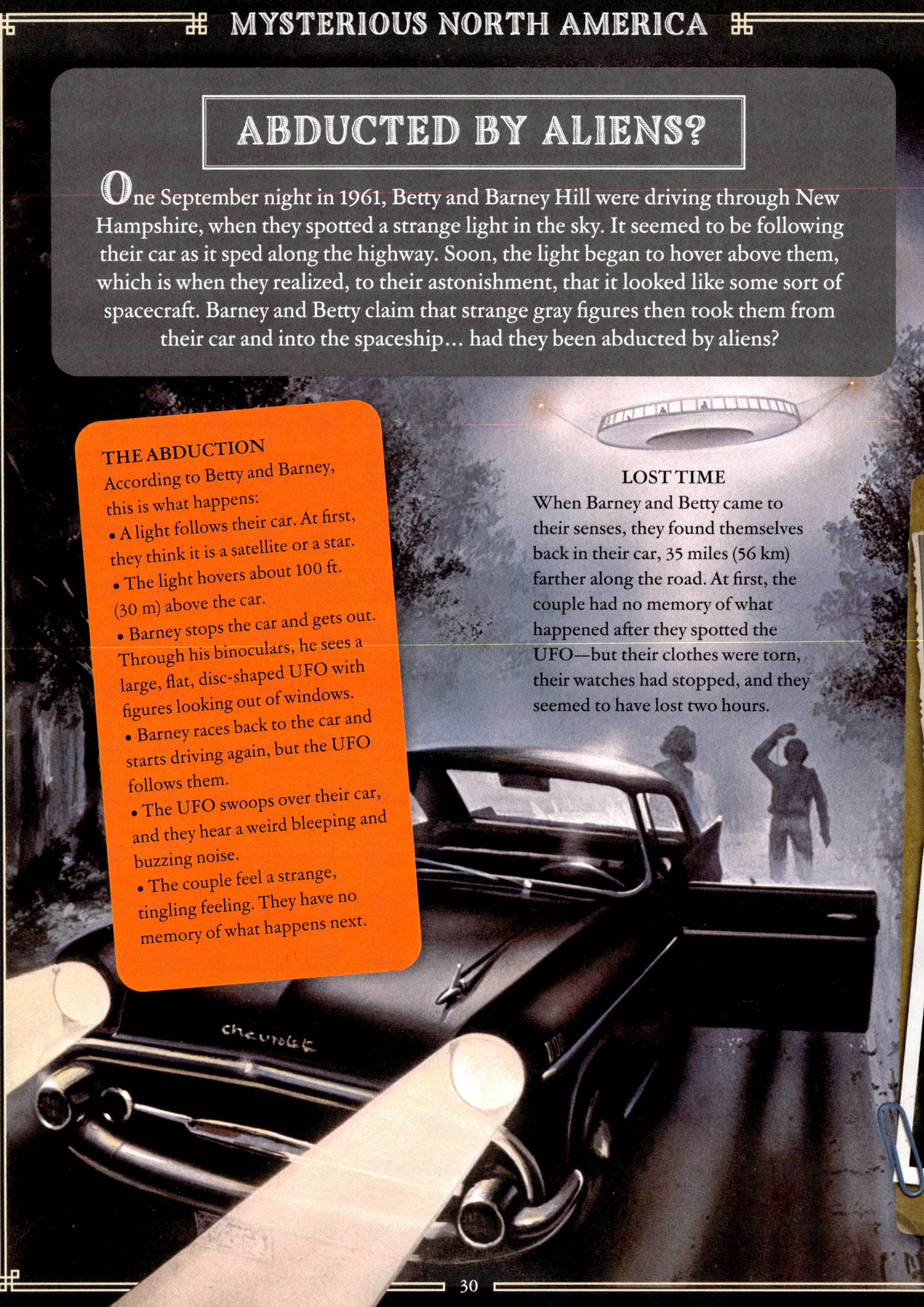

ABDUCTED BY ALIENS?

One September night in 1961, Betty and Barney Hill were driving through New Hampshire, when they spotted a strange light in the sky. It seemed to be following their car as it sped along the highway. Soon, the light began to hover above them, which is when they realized, to their astonishment, that it looked like some sort of spacecraft. Barney and Betty claim that strange gray figures then took them from their car and into the spaceship… had they been abducted by aliens?

THE ABDUCTION

According to Betty and Barney, this is what happens:

- A light follows their car. At first, they think it is a satellite or a star.
- The light hovers about 100 ft. (30 m) above the car.
- Barney stops the car and gets out. Through his binoculars, he sees a large, flat, disc-shaped UFO with figures looking out of windows.
- Barney races back to the car and starts driving again, but the UFO follows them.
- The UFO swoops over their car, and they hear a weird bleeping and buzzing noise.
- The couple feel a strange, tingling feeling. They have no memory of what happens next.

LOST TIME

When Barney and Betty came to their senses, they found themselves back in their car, 35 miles (56 km) farther along the road. At first, the couple had no memory of what happened after they spotted the UFO—but their clothes were torn, their watches had stopped, and they seemed to have lost two hours.

HYPNOSIS

After that night, Betty had nightmares about being abducted by aliens. But the couple still couldn't remember what happened to them. Three years later, they visited a doctor who used hypnosis to bring back Betty and Barney's memories. While hypnotized, they said that gray, human-like aliens took them into the spacecraft where they did tests on them and took samples of their hair, nails, and skin. Then the aliens put Barney and Betty back in their car.

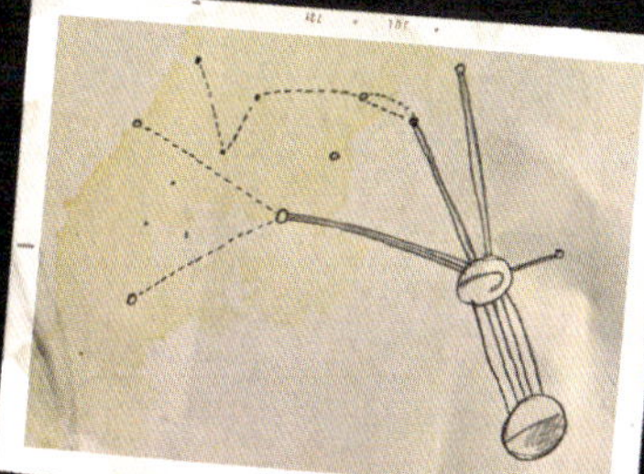

STAR MAP

Betty claimed that the aliens had shown her where they came from on a map of the stars. She later drew a copy of the map (left), which a teacher and amateur astronomer claimed matched the star system of Zeta Retuculi about 39 light-years from Earth. However, many scientists disagreed.

Is this the face of an alien? This is an artist's impression of one of the gray aliens based on Betty and Barney's descriptions. Barney also drew images of the spaceship (above).

WHAT COULD HAVE HAPPENED?

ALIEN CONTACT OR LIE?

Some people believe Betty and Barney really were abducted by aliens. Their stories matched each other's very closely, which would have been difficult if they'd made everything up. Other people think the story is nonsense. After all, there is no real evidence.

MIXED-UP DREAMS?

Betty had been having dreams about being abducted by aliens before she was hypnotized and might have told Barney about them. Could they have got confused about what was a memory and what was just a dream?

PROJECT BLUE BOOK

The US Air Force looked into Betty and Barney's claims that they were abducted by aliens. It was part of a secret study called Project Blue Book, investigating UFO sightings in the United States. The report said the UFO sighting was "probably" just an billboard spotlight. But many people think that was unlikely in the countryside where Barney and Betty were driving. Could the US Air Force have been covering up something strange and top secret, something they didn't want the public to know about?

AREA 51

Here's one location you won't be able to visit on vacation: Area 51. Often described as the "most secret place on Earth," this highly classified Air Force base in Nevada has long inspired conspiracy theories. Could it really be a warehouse filled with crashed UFOs and alien technology?

WHAT IS AREA 51?

This top-secret base covers a large, rectangular area in the state of Nevada, 23 by 25 miles (37 by 40 km). It sits next to a dry lake bed called Groom Lake, which is used as a natural aircraft runway. According to the US Air Force, Area 51 is a training range, and it's thought that experimental aircraft and weapons are developed and tested there by the US military.

STAY AWAY!

Area 51 was set up in 1955, but it was another 43 years before the US government admitted it existed. For many years, the base didn't appear on any maps, and even today only specially authorised military planes are allowed to fly over it. Members of the public are not allowed in. Outside the base are signs warning that "deadly force" could be used against trespassers. The edge of the base is protected by surveillance cameras, armed security guards, and buried motion sensors.

Satellite images of Area 51

WHAT'S RUMORED TO HAPPEN AT AREA 51?

According to many conspiracy theorists, the following takes place at the base:

- Storage and investigations of crashed alien spacecraft
- Designing aircraft based on materials from crashed spacecraft
- Study of alien bodies from crash landings
- Communication with aliens
- Development of new weapons based on alien technology
- Development of time machines and teleportation
- Filming the faked Moon landings

WHAT REALLY HAPPENS AT AREA 51?

According to the US Air Force, it's a place where new, cutting-edge aircraft and weapons are developed and tested, such as spy planes, stealth fighter planes, and drones. The US government keeps these top secret to stop any other countries stealing their ideas and inventions. People who have worked at Area 51 claim that many UFO sightings in the 1950s and beyond were actually people catching sight of new experimental aircraft.

The SR-71 "Blackbird" spy plane developed in secret in the early 1960s

UFO WITNESSES

A man named Bob Lazar claimed to be a scientist who worked at Area 51 in the 1980s. He said he saw at least nine different working alien spacecraft there, which had technology like nothing else he'd ever seen. However, there is evidence that Lazar may have lied about his education and career. Although he has some supporters, most people think his stories about what he saw at Area 51 were made up.

An artist's impression of scientists inspecting an alien craft in Area 51

MORE TO THE STORY?

With security around Area 51 kept so tight, it's impossible to know for sure what really goes on there. Whether you believe in aliens or not, it's clear that if you want to keep something secret, Area 51 is just the place to hide it...

HAUNTED NORTH AMERICA

In North America, you're never far from a creepy story of an unfortunate or mysterious death. From the wilds of Canada to the bustling cities of Mexico, ghosts haunt every corner of this spooky continent...

WINCHESTER MYSTERY

A creepy mansion in San Jose, California, is thought to be one of the most haunted houses in the United States. It was the home of Sallie Winchester (1831–1922), the widow of William Winchester (1837–1881), who made his fortune manufacturing guns. Sallie designed the mansion herself but kept adding new rooms and changing the layout. The house became a never-ending maze, with hundreds of rooms. Rumors grew that Sallie feared the house was haunted by the ghosts of people killed by her husband's guns and that she would die if the building work stopped.

A creepy light show is put on at the Winchester Mystery House every Halloween.

GHOSTS OR JOBS?

Today, tourists can visit the Winchester Mystery House to see the crazy architecture and try to catch a glimpse of the ghosts for themselves. However, Sallie Winchester's strange behavior might not have been given the credit it deserved. In a time when many people were poor and she was incredibly rich, it's been argued that she carried on building her grand mansion to give hundreds of local workers a well-paid job.

THE CHRISTMAS TREE SHIP

Every winter, the *Rouse Simmons*, also known as the "Christmas Tree Ship," would transport Christmas trees across Lake Michigan to sell in Chicago. The ship would be decked out with sparkling electric lights, bringing joy and excitement to the city. The captain, Herman Schuenemann, was lovingly nicknamed "Captain Santa." He would always give away some trees to struggling families to make sure everyone could celebrate.

Unfortunately, this festive cheer didn't last. On a stormy night in 1912, the beloved ship sank, drowning the captain and all on board. It became known in the city as "the year without Christmas." Since that time, a ghost ship carrying pine trees has been said to be seen out on the lake on Christmas Eve, and a phantom bell has been heard, ringing for the lost souls.

The captain's daughter Elsie continued to sell trees after the tragedy.

GHOST IN THE CANOE

If you visit Canoe Lake in Canada's Algonquin National Park, Ontario, you'll hear tales of a ghost who can be seen paddling in his canoe every year, around the anniversary of his death. This is said to be the spirit of the famous landscape artist Tom Thomson, who drowned while out on his canoe on July 8, 1917. Although it's thought that his death was accidental, no one can quite be sure. Perhaps that is why his restless ghost always seems to return to the lake where he died.

SUBWAY SPOOK

In a Mexico City subway station, there is rumored to be a friendly ghost. This spooky apparition is said to have died at the station while traveling alone, and has stuck around to help and protect other solo passengers. Would you like to receive help from a ghost?

PACAL THE GREAT

Around 1,400 years ago, Pacal the Great was the *ajaw*, or ruler, of the Maya city-state of Palenque in what is now Mexico. His rule lasted for 68 years—longer than any other king in the Americas. During that time, he oversaw incredible construction projects in the city. In recent times, however, he has become famous for a different reason. Since his tomb was discovered, its mysterious carved images have fascinated many people, with some claiming that they show evidence of an ancient astronaut in a spaceship.

AMAZING ARCHITECTURE

Hidden in the dense jungle of southern Mexico, Palenque was once a bustling city filled with buildings painted in bright red and blue. Even today, the stone ruins of Palenque's palace and temples seem extraordinary. They include huge, stepped pyramids and detailed wall carvings.

The towering Temple of the Inscriptions is now a tourist attraction.

DISCOVERING PACAL'S TOMB

Pacal came to the throne in 615 CE, aged just 12 years old. He ruled until his death, aged 80. He was then buried in a sarcophagus in Palenque's largest pyramid, known as the Temple of the Inscriptions. The secret opening to the tomb was only discovered in 1948. It took another four years to clear away all the rubble so archaeologists could get into it. It was worth the wait...

Are the figure's hands operating the controls of a spaceship, and are those exhaust flames?

THE MASK OF PACAL

Finally, in 1952, archaeologists entered the tomb. They found it undisturbed. The walls were covered in sculptures, and at the tomb's center stood the sarcophagus of the king. Pacal's skeleton was still inside, wearing a beautiful mask and necklaces made of green jade.

"It looked like a magic cave sculpted out of ice, the walls shimmering and bright like crystals of snow." —archaeologist Alberto Ruz's description of entering the tomb for the first time.

ALIEN ASTRONAUT

The image on the lid of Pacal's sarcophagus (above) has proved very intriguing since it was uncovered. Some people have claimed that it clearly shows an ancient astronaut blasting off into space in a rocket. They think it reveals that aliens came to Earth thousands of years ago, helping the Maya people to build their amazing structures using technology and skills from outer space.

ENTERING THE AFTERLIFE

Archaeologists don't believe the sarcophagus shows an astronaut. They say that the carvings show Pacal being reborn as a god in the afterlife. Furthermore, they say the king is on his back looking upward, not side on, and the "rocket's fire" is, in fact, a mythical water serpent representing the entrance to the underworld. Above Pacal is the World Tree, another important image in Maya art that symbolized the creation of the Earth and sky.

IS IT FAIR?

Claiming that aliens helped the Maya to build Palenque and other cities suggests we don't think the people who lived there could have done it on their own. Shouldn't we give the ancient Maya credit for their achievements? Or does the carving make you wonder if there might be something in the claims of alien help?

CHUPACABRA

If you go down to the woods today, you better not go alone… if the stories are to be believed, you might just come across the deadly Chupacabra. "Chupacabra" means "goat-sucker" in Spanish, and that's exactly what this vampire-like monster is said to do: suck the blood from goats and other farm animals.

MODERN MONSTERS

Tales of the dreaded Chupacabra only began in 1995, when it was first supposedly spotted in Puerto Rico, a US island in the Caribbean. There were more than 200 reports of the Chupacabra in Puerto Rico at that time. Since then, sightings have spread to the mainland United States' as well as to parts of Mexico.

CHANGING DESCRIPTIONS

Early reports in Puerto Rico described the Chupacabra as standing on two legs and about 3 ft. (1 m) tall. It is said to have spikes down its back, short gray fur, long fangs, and even glowing-red eyes. Some described it as hopping like a kangaroo. However, more recent sightings in the US and Mexico describe the creature as being doglike, walking on four legs, and sometimes hairless. Could these really be the same creature?

WHAT COULD IT BE?

SICK COYOTES?

People who think they've seen the Chupacabra might actually have spotted coyotes or stray dogs with a skin infection called mange. This can make the animals lose their fur and develop sore, scaly skin. If a coyote is sick and weak, it would struggle to hunt wild prey and might start trying to attack farm animals instead. Some photos said to show dead Chupacabra have been proven to be coyotes with very bad mange.

HAIRLESS DOGS?

A sick coyote could explain some of the sightings on mainland USA, but there are no coyotes in Puerto Rico. Perhaps it could have been a hairless dog instead. There are certain types of dogs found in Peru and Mexico that have been bred not to have hair. The "monster" sightings could have been one of these rare breeds seen in an unfamiliar setting.

MOVIE MADNESS?

The first reports of a goat-sucking monster in Puerto Rico happened around the same time that the horror film *Species* was released in the mid-1990s. The film featured an alien that looked suspiciously like the alleged Chupacabra. Could people have started imagining they had seen something similar on the loose in their neighborhood?

MONKEY MAYHEM?

Another theory is that people in Puerto Rico were seeing a group of rhesus monkeys that had escaped from a lab. Rhesus monkeys can stand on their back legs, have gray fur, and their canine teeth look a lot like fangs—quite a scary sight if you're not expecting it!

WAMPUS CAT

The Chupacabra isn't the only strange creature thought to menace North America. According to Cherokee folklore, the Wampus Cat was a woman who was transformed into a monster by a medicine man as punishment for watching a sacred ceremony. The Wampus Cat is said to stalk the Appalachian Mountains, and has been blamed for killing farm animals. Like a sort of giant, magical mountain lion, it is often depicted as having six legs.

THE STONE SPHERES OF COSTA RICA

If you could step back in time 1,000 years and visit Central America, you might find people making some very curious objects: perfectly round stone spheres. When the area was invaded by the Spanish Empire in the early 16th century, the spheres were forgotten. For centuries they lay hidden beneath a tropical jungle. When they were finally rediscovered, nobody had a clue where they came from, or what they were for...

WHAT ARE THEY?

The mysterious objects are more than 300 stone balls of different sizes. Some of the balls are just an inch or so wide, while the biggest measures more than 8.2 ft. (2.5 m) across and weighs 16 tons. Most are carved from a hard type of rock called gabbro, but some are made from softer limestone or sandstone.

The Diquis also made intricate jewelry, like this gold pendant.

HOW WERE THEY MADE?

We're still not sure exactly how these mysterious stones were created. Archaeologists think they were probably carved from giant boulders, hammered and shaped with other rocks and then polished with sand, but no one knows how each was made into an almost perfectly spherical shape. One thing is for sure, though: a lot of work and skill must have gone into making them and moving them to their locations.

WHO MADE THEM?

The stone spheres were discovered on a delta (a place where a river meets the sea) on the west coast of Costa Rica as well as on a small offshore island. The earliest stones were likely made around 600 CE, but most were probably made after 1000 CE. They are thought to have been made by the Diquis people, who lived in the area. Sadly, very little is known about this culture as it went extinct when the Spanish conquered Central America.

WHY WERE THE SPHERES MADE?

SIGNS OF POWER?

Experts think the stones were placed in lines going up to chiefs' houses. Maybe they were a symbol of how rich and powerful the chiefs were.

SKY STONES?

Some archaeologists think the spheres might have represented the Solar System, the Sun rising and setting, or the phases of the Moon.

A WORK OF NATURE?

A few people insist that the stones are natural, not human-made. But nothing like these stones has been found elsewhere in nature.

MAGIC POTION?

There is a legend that the people who created the spheres used a magic potion to soften the rock. Although it is possible that some of the limestone rock could have been dissolved with acid made from plants, it still seems like an unlikely story. Acid wouldn't have worked well on most of the spheres, which were made from hard gabbro rock.

GOLDEN CENTER

The spheres were rediscovered nearly 100 years ago, when the land was cleared to grow bananas. The people clearing the jungle had heard stories of hidden treasure, and they thought there might be gold inside the balls. They drilled holes into some of them and blew other ones apart with sticks of dynamite, but there was no gold inside. Today, the stone spheres are protected as important artifacts from the past.

THE AURORA BOREALIS

If you travel to the far north of the continent, you might be lucky enough to see the greatest light show on Earth dancing across the night sky. Today, scientists can explain this awe-inspiring natural phenomenon, but cultures across the world once told stories of gods, heroes, and magical animals to make sense of the beautiful aurora borealis.

FRIENDLY OR FEARSOME?

There are almost as many different stories explaining the lights as there are cultures:

- SPIRITS OF THE DEAD – In some cultures, such as the Cree tribes in Canada, the lights are traditionally explained as being the souls of people's ancestors.
- FIERY FOX – In Finland, a legend tells how the lights were caused by a magical fox flicking crystals of snow into the sky with its tail. The Finnish word for the "aurora," *revontulet*, means "fox fires."
- FIRE LIGHT –Some Anishinaabe peoples of Canada tell a story of how the light came from a huge fire built by the world's creator, Nanabozho, to show those down on Earth that he was thinking of them.
- GLITTERING FISHES – Swedish fishermen once interpreted the lights as the reflections of giant schools of herring. They thought seeing the lights was a lucky omen, guaranteeing them a good catch.

WHAT REALLY CAUSES THE AURORA?

The scientific explanation for the aurora borealis was first proposed by the Norwegian scientist Kristian Birkeland (1867–1917)—and is just as amazing as the myths. Electrically charged particles from the Sun are captured by the Earth's magnetic field. They crash into gas atoms in Earth's atmosphere, heating them up and making them glow. Earth's magnetic field is strongest near the North and South Poles, so that is where the auroras are most visible.

Birkeland (left) created a terrella, a magnetized model of the Earth to show how its auroras form.

THE SAILING STONES

How could a heavy lump of rock move by itself? For years, this was a mystery that puzzled all who saw the "sailing stones" in Death Valley, California. The rocks appeared to have traveled across flat, dry lake beds, leaving long tracks behind them in the hard earth. But there was no evidence that anyone was doing the moving—no footprints or tire marks. The stones seemed to be moving themselves. But surely that was impossible?

NO ANSWERS

For decades, scientists studied the sailing stones, taking measurements and monitoring the conditions. Still, they could only guess what was moving the stones. They thought that perhaps strong winds were responsible, but could wind really be strong enough to push giant rocks around? Not everyone thought so.

GUESSING GAME

Some people came up with other explanations for the wandering rocks:

- Aliens
- Pranksters
- Unexplained magnetic forces

WHAT REALLY MOVES THE STONES?

New technology finally helped solve the mystery. Time-lapse photography and GPS transmitters allowed scientists to discover that the stones were being moved by large, thin ice sheets. These ice sheets formed when the lake bed flooded in winter. During cold winter nights, the ice froze hard, but then began breaking up on sunny mornings. The wind moved the thawing ice sheets, and the ice dragged the rocks with them.

SOUTH AMERICA

Once home to the prosperous Inca Empire, South America has seen many explorers disappear into its jungles on a quest to find legendary gold. From the puzzling Nazca Lines to the extraordinary stonework of Pumapunku, the mountains, rainforests, and deserts of this southern continent hold many ancient secrets waiting to be unraveled. But some of its mysteries have left little trace—those searching for Brazil's fabled Mapinguari or evidence of a UFO crash are likely to find only whispers and rumors.

KEY

Would you battle through the crocodile-filled waters of the Amazon basin or climb the rugged, frozen peaks of Patagonia to track down answers to South America's mysteries?

1
2
3
4
5
6
7
8
9
10
11
12
13
14
15
16
N
W
E
S

EL DORADO

When Spanish explorers reached South America in the 1500s, they found civilisations with an abundance of gold. Rumor spread that somewhere in South America was a secret land that held unimaginable riches. It became known as El Dorado. Despite countless attempts to find this "Lost City of Gold," it was never tracked down. Was it just a myth or could there really be a treasure trove of gold, forgotten somewhere in the remote jungle?

An example of Inca goldwork

An intricate gold artifact has been found that depicts the ritual at Lake Guatavita. It was discovered in a small cave in Colombia in 1969.

THE MEANING OF GOLD

In South American cultures, gold was used as decoration and for religious offerings rather than for money. Spanish conquistadors (conquerors) thought that if the Inca and other civilisations showed off that much gold, then they must have unimaginable riches hidden away.

LAKE OF GOLD

Legend told of the sacred Lake Guatavita, high in the Andes mountains in what is now Colombia. Each time a new local chieftain was crowned, he was covered in gold dust and would dive from a raft into the lake. Objects made of gold and precious stones would be thrown into the lake as a gift to the gods. The Spanish eventually found the lake in 1537 and tried to drain it. They managed to remove enough water to find hundreds of golden treasures around the edge of the lake but they could never reach the bottom to discover what riches might be hidden there.

Archaeologists have found evidence of golden offerings in Lake Guatavita (above), so the legend of the lake might well be true.

An artistic impression of a city of gold believed by some Spanish colonists to be hidden in Colombia's jungles

This historical illustration shows a conquistador carrying off an immense golden vase. Thousands of Europeans were lured to the region with dreams of incredible wealth.

A PLACE OR A PERSON?

The name El Dorado means "The Golden One" in Spanish. It was originally the name given to the chieftain who covered himself in gold at Lake Guatavita, but over time it began to be used as the name for the legendary lost city.

OTHER MYTHICAL CITIES

El Dorado wasn't the only legendary city thought to be hidden somewhere in South America:

- Explorers searched in vain for the City of the Caesars—also known as the Wandering City—a mythical and fabulously wealthy place said to be somewhere between Chile and Argentina in the far south of the continent.
- The mythical Inca city of Paititi was also fabled to lie hidden deep in the rainforest somewhere around Peru, Bolivia, or northwest Brazil. According to legend, it is where the last of the Inca retreated to when Spanish invaders took over their territories.

MELTING THE GOLD

Today, looters still hunt for lost treasures. Sadly, they often care only about the value of the gold. The fascinating artifacts are melted down, destroying the stories they could have told us about the cultures that made them.

STILL SEARCHING

It is clear that South Americans were creating many wonderful golden objects around the time that Spanish conquistadors came to the continent. Over the centuries, many have hunted for lost treasures—and found them—but so far, no one has been able to track down a lost city of gold.

NAZCA LINES

If you fly over an area of desert in southern Peru, you'll see an amazing sight below you: giant pictures carved into the ground. These large land images are known as the Nazca Lines after the ancient Nazca people who created them. They were clearly designed to be seen from far above, but by whom? Gods? Aliens? They were created over more than a thousand years, from around 500 BCE to 500 CE, and incredibly, they are still visible all these years later.

LOOKING FOR LINES

Before the use of airplanes, it was very difficult to see most of the designs. The best way of viewing them was from the surrounding foothills. In recent years, archaeologists have been able to discover and record many more by using drones to photograph and film them. There are hundreds of designs in total.

This image shows a collection of the giant images. In reality, the images are much more spaced out.

Each Nazca image was created by removing lines of reddish pebbles on the surface of the desert in order to reveal the lighter-colored earth underneath. Because the lines are in a dry and sheltered location, most of them have been naturally preserved.

A NAZCA ZOO

Some of the most exciting and recognizable pictures—technically known as geoglyphs—are of animals, including a hummingbird, a monkey, a spider, a condor, a pelican, a cat, a dog, a lizard, a fish, a killer whale, and many more. Many of the designs are more than 160 ft. (50 m) across and, together, all the Nazca lines cover an area of around 170 square miles (450 sq km).

WHY WERE THEY MADE?

MESSAGES FOR THE GODS?

Archaeologists are still trying to figure out why the Nazca people made such huge drawings in the earth. Some think it might have been for religious reasons, perhaps as an offering to the gods looking down from the sky. They might have been used as part of a religious ceremony, possibly to ask the gods to bless their land with rain.

ALIENS?

Some people have suggested that the Nazca Lines are too sophisticated to have been created by the cultures of the past. Instead, they argue "alien astronauts" came to Earth thousands of years ago. They brought advanced technology, which they shared with ancient peoples who used them to build incredible structures, such as the Nazca Lines.

AN ANCIENT CALENDAR?

There are Nazca Lines that mark the position of the Sun during the summer and winter solstices (the longest and shortest days of the year). This has led some experts to think that perhaps they were used to keep track of important points in the year, like a big calendar carved into the ground. But if that's the case, it doesn't explain all the images.

The Nazca were capable of creating sophisticated pottery, so why not larger works?

...OR JUST REGULAR PEOPLE?

Archaeologists who have studied the Nazca Lines say that there is no evidence of alien astronauts. Instead, they argue that the skill and knowledge of ancient peoples should not be underestimated. In fact, in 1982, a US investigator named Joe Nickell recreated one of the images using the same simple tools that would have been available to the Nazca people. He did this to show that they could be made by a small team of people in just a few days. But that only explains that they could be made, not why they were made. What do you think?

MAPINGUARI

The dark, damp Amazon rainforest is home to many strange—and sometimes dangerous—creatures. Far from any towns and cities, there is much in the dense jungle that still hasn't been fully explored. What better place than this for the monstrous and foul-smelling spirit known as the Mapinguari to lurk?

RAINFOREST PROTECTOR

The Mapinguari features in the folklore of many Brazilian Indigenous groups. According to one legend, the Mapinguari was once a shaman who angered the gods by discovering the secret of immortality. As punishment, they turned him into a bloodthirsty monster, destined to roam the jungle forever. In other versions of the tale, the Mapinguari is viewed as a protector of the rainforest who attacks greedy hunters and trespassers. Its legend can be seen as a warning to those who destroy the precious Amazon rainforest.

What does it look (and smell) like?

- One huge eye in the middle of its forehead
- A giant mouth in the middle of its belly
- Walks on all fours but can rear up and walk on two
- The height of a man when upright, sometimes taller
- Feet that are turned backward or inward, leaving confusing tracks
- Reddish fur and tough skin that protect it from attack
- Gives off a disgusting smell, powerful enough to knock a person out

SIGHTINGS

Hundreds of people have reported seeing a Mapinguari, catching a whiff of its foul stench, or witnessing the trail of destruction left behind as it lumbers through the jungle. However, no one has yet discovered any physical evidence to suggest such a fearsome monster actually exists.

WHAT COULD IT BE?

BIGFOOT'S COUSIN?

Stories about Mapinguari have been passed down for centuries within native Brazilian communities, but it was usually seen as a mythical spirit rather than as a real beast. However, when stories were shared with European and North American cryptozoologists in the 20th century, they started thinking that the mythical creature might in fact be an unknown ape-like creature, like Bigfoot (page 18).

GIANT SLOTH?

A new theory took hold in the 1990s. A scientist called Dr. David Oren thought that descriptions of the Mapinguari sounded similar to a giant ground sloth, known as a megatherium, that once lived in South America (above). However, it went extinct thousands of years ago—and it never had a gaping mouth in the middle of its belly. Dr. Oren thought the legend might have begun when early peoples in the Amazon came into contact with the last remaining giant ground sloths.

LOST IN THE JUNGLE?

Some people think that a few giant ground sloths might still be roaming the rainforest and that's what people are spotting when they think they've seen a Mapinguari. If that's true, it seems strange that no evidence of living giant sloths has been found: after all, they are giant. But then again, the jungle is huge...

UFO CRASH LANDING

Did an alien craft crash-land in Brazil in the 1990s? There are certainly many in the town of Varginha who are convinced it did, and that some of the townspeople even had encounters with the aliens that emerged. The authorities have denied such an event took place, but are they covering up the truth...?

WHAT HAPPENED?

- January 13, 1996 – It's claimed that the US Air Force shot down a UFO, which crashed near Varginha in southeast Brazil.
- January 20, 1996 – Two sisters, aged 14 and 16, and their 21-year-old friend saw a strange creature hunched near the site. They ran away in terror. When they got home, they said that they had seen a devil.
- They returned to the site with their mother, where they saw a strange, three-toed footprint. For days after, they could smell a horrible stench, like rotten eggs, but worse.
- According to some reports, after the crash, the local fire department captured two unidentified creatures. One officer was scratched and became ill.

An artist's impression of a UFO crash-landing in the jungle

UFO WRECK

Professor (and amateur pilot) Carlos de Sousa claimed to have seen the UFO crash. According to de Sousa, the UFO was the shape of a submarine and about the size of a school bus, with white smoke billowing out as it fell through the sky. He ran to the crash site, but soldiers arrived and ordered him to leave.

WHAT DID THE "ALIEN" LOOK LIKE?

- According to the three girls, the two-legged creature had a large head with "spots like veins on the skin and some bumps on the head." Its eyes were "two red balls."
- They thought that the creature seemed sick or injured, describing it as "shrunken" and appearing to be "suffering from the heat."
- The older girl recalled that "what I saw stopped me in my tracks … It glued me to that spot. It had red eyes, oily skin. I couldn't see an open mouth. Not smiling… Sad expression. Shrunken back. It didn't have hair. Eyes three times bigger than ours."
- The middle child, Lilliane, said: "What we saw wasn't human and wasn't an animal either. Nowadays, I do think it was a being from another planet."

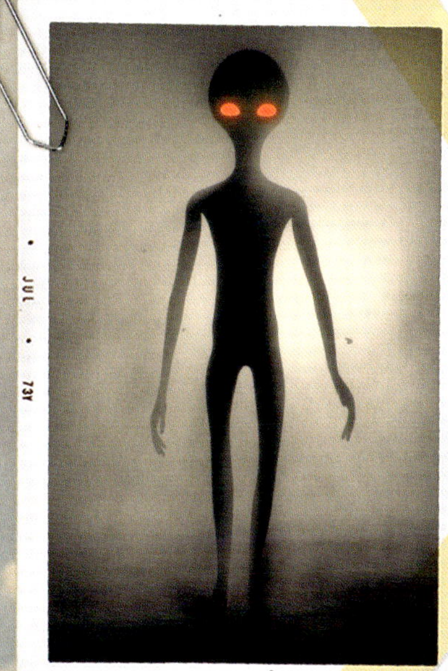

ALIEN INFECTION

Soon, news about the suspected alien encounter gripped the town. When a young military officer died a few weeks later, rumors spread that he had touched one of the alien bodies and had become infected with a deadly disease.

MILITARY REPORT

With rumors spreading and excitement growing, the military investigated the extraterrestrial claims. Their report gave explanations for each event and concluded that no aliens had crashed in Brazil. Despite this, many UFOlogists continue to believe that a UFO crashed and that several injured aliens were captured by the military. Today, there is no evidence other than eyewitness statements. Could the whole thing have been covered up, or was it a case of mistaken identity and wild imaginations?

The town's water tower is built in the shape of a UFO in reference to the incident.

PUMAPUNKU

Near the city of Tiwanaku in Bolivia lie some perplexing ruins. A great temple erected in the sixth century CE, Pumapunku has so far not revealed the mystery of how it was made. Was this incredible feat of architecture the work of skilled craftspeople… or perhaps visitors from another planet?

INCREDIBLE SKILL

Pumapunku might seem like any other ruin, except for its mysterious stone blocks. These huge blocks were cut with such incredible precision that they fitted together like a puzzle. No mortar was needed to stick them together. The surface of the blocks was polished to make them extremely smooth. How could ancient people have created something so exact without modern technology? So far, no one has discovered the kinds of tools used to carve the mysterious stones.

These intricate shapes carved into the stones show the incredible skill of the people who made them.

ALIEN ARCHITECTS?

Some people argue that Pumapunku's precise stonework was so advanced that it couldn't have been built by the people of the time. They think that ancient aliens must have either built it or provided advanced technology such as lasers, teaching the locals how to create the incredible buildings. But no one can answer how (or why) aliens would do such a thing.

WHAT WAS PUMAPUNKU?

Pumapunku would have been a very important spiritual place within the Tiwanaku Empire. Thought to have been built around 1,400 years ago, it was a large temple complex made up of earth platforms, buildings, stairways, gateways, and courtyards. Although it looks like lumps of ruined stones now, when it was new it was probably covered in brightly colored decorations of silver and gold.

Reconstruction of a 2,000-year-old archway at Tiwanaku

CONCRETE EVIDENCE

A few people studying Pumapunku think that some of the blocks—particularly some interesting H-shaped blocks—are not carved from stone at all. Instead, tests show they may have been made from an ancient sort of concrete, poured into molds to create the precision shapes.

MOVING THE MEGA BLOCKS

Some of the blocks are absolutely huge. The largest are nearly 26 ft. (8 m) long, 16 ft. (5 m) wide, and 3 ft. (1 m) thick, and weigh 144 tons. Scientists have figured out that the stone came from a quarry about 6 miles (10 km) away, near Lake Titicaca. No one can answer how the builders managed to transport such heavy blocks up a steep slope to the temple site.

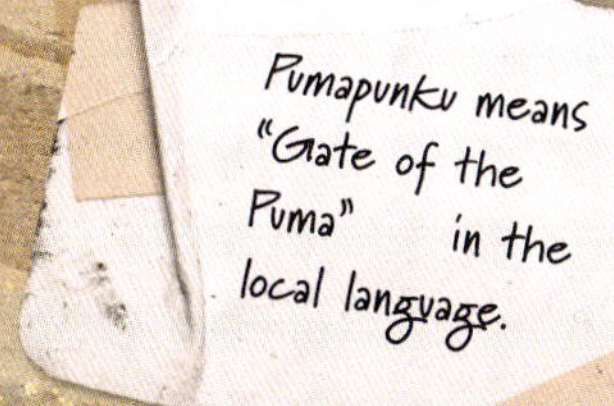

Pumapunku means "Gate of the Puma" in the local language.

Archaeologists and scientists continue to study Pumapunku. Perhaps, one day, they will finally unlock the mystery of how an ancient culture created such a masterpiece.

DESTROYED

Pumapunku may have been destroyed by an earthquake. Although some of the walls are still standing, many of the ruins are scattered about, making it difficult to piece them back together to glimpse what the place once looked like. However, archaeologists have used 3D-printing technology to create a reconstruction.

THE DEVIL'S LAGOON

In Chile's Atacama Desert, one of the world's driest places, any water is a welcome sight for travelers. But the Laguna Roja (red lagoon), located high up in a remote part of the desert, is no gentle, cooling oasis. Instead, you will find a steaming cauldron of blood-red liquid. Until recently, only the local people knew of this creepy sight, and their eerie stories only add to the mystery.

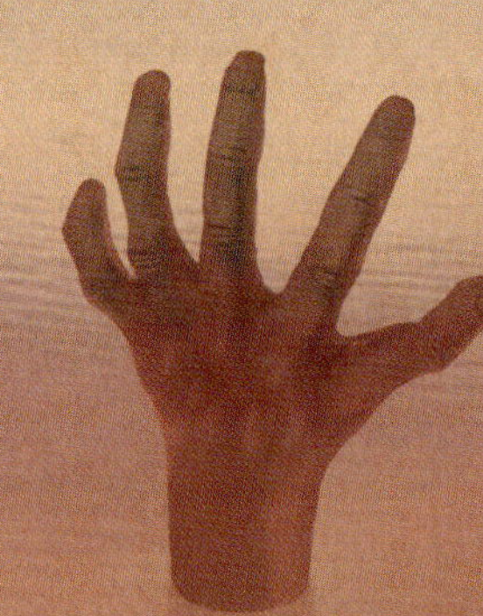

CURSED WATER

According to the region's Aymara people, the water is cursed. Legend has it that the lake belongs to the Devil. To keep people away, he stained it red as a warning, and it has grown a deeper shade each time someone has drunk the deadly water. Many people believe the lagoon still has a sinister power and continue to keep their distance.

The lake is said to be responsible for the mysterious disappearance of several people.

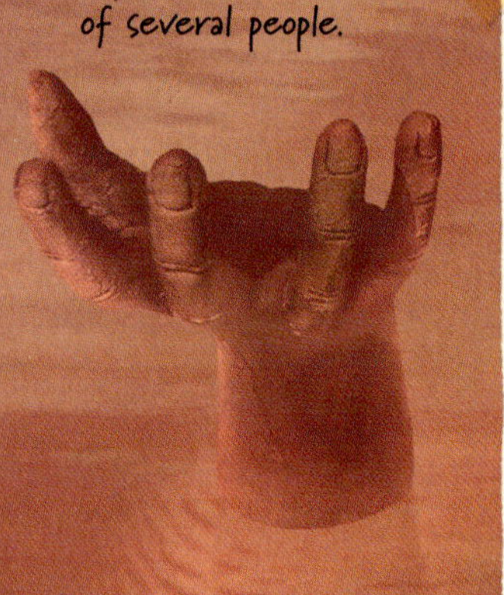

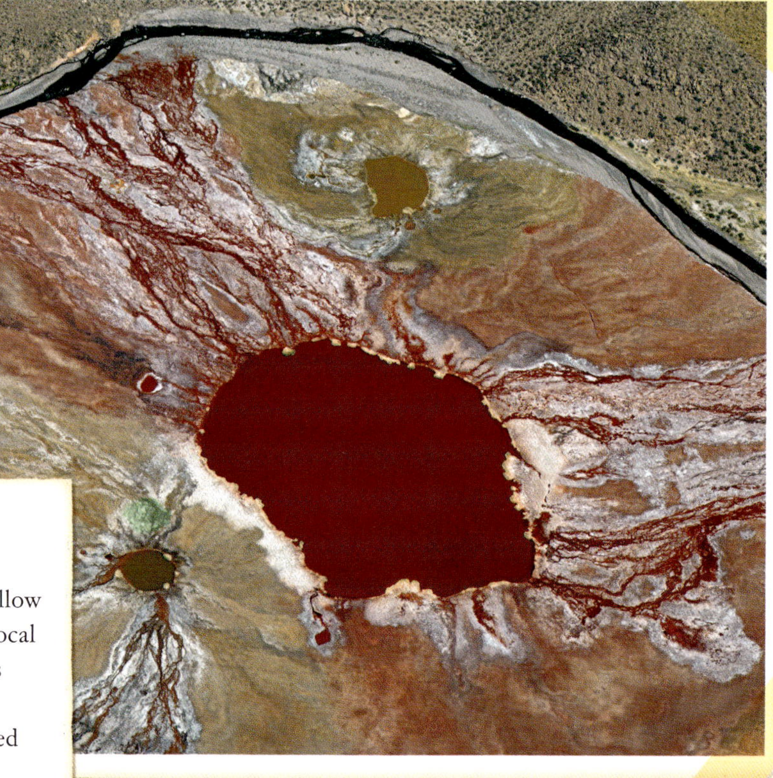

TRIO OF TEARS

Nearby are two other brightly colored lagoons, one a vivid yellow and the other green. Another local legend tells that the three lakes were formed from the tears of three people who were sacrificed to the gods long ago.

WHAT IS TURNING THE WATER RED?

ALGAE?

Though superstition has long surrounded the red lagoon, scientists think they might have found a reason for its sinister appearance. It's likely that the red color is caused by algae and sediments deep in the lake. Perhaps the true reason for the lagoon's devilish reputation should be its super-salty, scalding water. With temperatures reaching 120°F (50°C), it's too hot for most animals to survive there.

COLORFUL COMPANY

Laguna Roja's blood-red waters are impressive, but they aren't one of a kind. South America is lucky enough to have a few amazing lakes in different shades. It's thought that different minerals, bacteria, and algae produce the range of strange colors.

Like Laguna Roja, Laguna Colorada's colour is caused by algae in the water.

Laguna Pujsa in northern Chile is a toxic-looking yellow.
Laguna Colorada in Bolivia is a rusty red.
Laguna Verde in Bolivia is a turquoise green.

Both beautiful and deadly, Laguna Verde's bright green color is the result of high levels of lead, sulphur, and arsenic in the water.

HAUNTED SOUTH AMERICA

On November 1st and 2nd each year, many South Americans remember their lost loved ones by celebrating the Day of the Dead. But for those unlucky souls that don't rest in peace, it seems that any time of year is a good time to haunt the living. Throughout this southern continent, you'll hear whispered stories of ghostly sightings…

LA NORIA CEMETERY, CHILE

In the bone-dry Atacama Desert of Chile lies a cemetery where you might just stumble over bones. La Noria was once a bustling center of mining, but after the mines closed, it was deserted, becoming a ghost town. The cemetery is now in ruins, with many coffins lying open. Those who are brave—or stupid—enough to visit the graveyard at night tell of hearing strange footsteps and seeing shadows rising from the graves to wander the town. After their hard lives toiling in the mines, the ghosts are thought to be angry that their final resting place has been disturbed.

The graves lie abandoned and decaying under the fierce desert Sun.

HOTEL DEL SALTO, COLOMBIA

One hundred years ago, the del Salto was a luxury hotel with an unbeatable view. Perched on the edge of the Tequendama waterfall, the hotel's rich visitors could look down as the tumbling white waters fell 512 ft. (156 m) below. Unfortunately, the pull of the waterfall was too great for some, with more than 20 people thought to have jumped to their death. In the years afterward, ghostly cries have been heard, said to be from the spirits of those who took their own life. The creepy hotel was eventually abandoned and is now a museum.

DREAM BEACH, BRAZIL

Though this stretch of coast in Itanhaém, São Paulo, might be beautiful by day, visitors and coastguards claim to have seen unsettling visions by night. According to the locals, two bedraggled and gruesome ghosts are sometimes seen walking out of the surf. They are thought to be the restless spirits of a couple who were dragged into the sea by a freak wave while taking a moonlit walk and whose bodies were never found. Eerie whispers and blood-chilling screams have also been heard along the rocky shore.

THE HAUNTED HUT, ECUADOR

High on the snowy slopes of Chimborazo, a dormant volcano in Ecuador, you'll find a simple hut waiting to greet mountaineers on their journey to the summit. But while the hut might offer welcome refuge from the cold, it also has some frights in store for anyone who stays the night. Mountain guides claim to have felt ghostly presences in the hut, including being slapped on the back and being pulled out of bed when no one else was there. It's thought the spooky happenings might be the work of climbers who have died on the perilous volcano.

LA RECOLETA CEMETERY, ARGENTINA

At this famous cemetery in Buenos Aires, the ghost of a girl named Rufina Cambaceres is regularly spotted. She died suddenly in 1902 and was buried here. But when her tomb was visited a few weeks later by workers, they found the coffin had moved. Opening it up, they discovered scratch marks on the coffin lid. It appeared that Rufina hadn't died at all, but had merely fainted. She had then awoken and tried to claw her way out before having a fatal heart attack. A marble statue of Rufina now stands at the tomb entrance (right), making sure she can come and go as she pleases.

THE EVERLASTING LIGHTNING STORM

Take a nighttime visit to a swampy corner of Venezuela, where the Catatumbo River meets Lake Maracaibo, and you're likely to see one of the most spectacular light shows on Earth. This is the location of the "everlasting" lightning storm where there are around 1.2 million lightning flashes every year. For centuries, this phenomenon has puzzled spectators and scientists alike.

A DAZZLING DISPLAY

During the rainy season, lightning strikes shoot down for nine or ten hours each night. This happens on around 160 nights a year, and sometimes on as many as 300 nights a year. Lightning strikes hit the area 16 to 40 times per minute, giving Catatumbo the Guinness World Record for the highest concentration of lightning in the world.

Catatumbo means "House of Thunder" in the language of the local Barí people.

THE ANSWER IS BLOWING IN THE WIND

For years, scientists couldn't explain what created so much lightning. We now know it's caused by particular conditions in the atmosphere. Warm, damp winds from the Caribbean Sea off the shore of Venezuela build up an intense electrical charge. This charge is released as a flurry of lightning bolts when it reaches the coast and meets cold air from the surrounding mountains.

GLOWING TERMITE MOUNDS

South America is home to more than one magnificent light display. In parts of Emas National Park in Brazil, the termite mounds light up like a forest of Christmas trees at the start of the rainy season. It is said that when settlers first arrived here, they were afraid of the glowing mounds. They thought that the towering piles of earth contained spirits. It took many years before scientists figured out the truth.

ANTEATER TREATS

During the day and outside the rainy season, the mounds are not illuminated. These giant structures can be over 10 ft. (3 m) tall and are home to hundreds of thousands of insects. For giant anteaters, which feast on termites, the mounds are an irresistible buffet. They use their long claws to tear the mounds open and get at the termites within, which they lap up with their super-long tongue.

SOLVED

Thousands of glowing larvae create a twinkling tapestry across the grassland.

WHAT'S GLOWING?

The beautiful green glow that speckles the termite mounds at night isn't caused by spirits or any other mystical being. It isn't even caused by the termites that build the mounds. It is produced by the larvae of the click beetle, also known as the headlight beetle. The glow-in-the-dark larvae burrow into the outside of the termite mounds and shine to attract flying insect prey—including the termites whose house they are staying in!

The adult beetles also glow from two spots just behind their head.

EUROPE

Though Europe is one of the smallest continents, it has some of the biggest mysteries. From the jaw-dropping architecture of Stonehenge in England to a mind-boggling bronze computer from ancient Greece, it's clear that early Europeans had knowledge that we struggle to explain. And with so much history, it's no surprise that ghosts are said to dwell in many of the castles that dot the landscape. Today, Europe is full of towns, cities and farmland. Though few big, wild animals still roam the land, sightings of the legendary Loch Ness Monster and the Beast of Bodmin Moor suggest we might just need to keep our eyes open.

KEY

1. Bloody Square – Stockholm, Sweden, p.85
2. Ring of Brodgar – Orkney, Scotland, UK, p.72
3. Missing Lighthouse Keepers – Flannan Lighthouse Eilean Mòr, Outer Hebrides, Scotland, UK, p.64
4. Loch Ness Monster – Scotland, UK, p.66
5. Dancing Forest – Kaliningrad, Russia, p.86
6. Malahide Castle – County Dublin, Ireland, p.84
7. Punchestown Longstone – County Kildare, Ireland, p.73
8. Crooked Forest – Poland, p.86
9. Roman Dodecahedrons – Western Europe, p.83
10. Stonehenge – Wiltshire, England, UK, p.70
11. Crop Circles – Southwest England, UK, p.89
12. Beast of Bodmin Moor – Bodmin Moor, Cornwall, England, UK, p.74
13. Tolvan Holed Stone – Cornwall, England, UK, p.73
14. Zvikov Castle – Czech Republic, p.84
15. Paris Catacombs – Paris, France, p.85
16. Carnac Stones – Brittany, France, p.73
17. Tatzelwurm – The Alps, p.76
18. Haunted Forest – Hoia Baciu, Romania, p.78
19. Voynich Manuscript – Italy, p.80
20. Colosseum – Rome, Italy, p.85
21. Dolmen of Guadalperal – Spain, p.72
22. Blue Grotto – Capri, Italy, p.88
23. Antikythera Mechanism – Antikythera, Greece, p.82

Dozens of mysterious Roman dodecahedrons have been unearthed in Western Europe (page 83). Could you be the person to find the next one?
1
2
3
4
5
6
7
8
9
10
11
12
13
14
15
16
17
18
19
20
21
22
23

THE MISSING LIGHTHOUSE KEEPERS

The Flannan Isles Lighthouse is perched on the highest point of Eilean Mòr, a tiny, remote island off the northwest coast of Scotland. Here, the weather can turn nasty in an instant, with pounding rain and massive waves that crash against the rocks. In the past, the only people who stayed on Eilean Mòr were the lighthouse keepers. They made sure the huge oil lamp remained lit to warn boats away from the rocks. But in 1900, just a year after the lighthouse was built, the light went out. All three lighthouse keepers had vanished.

The three lighthouse keepers who went missing (from the left): Thomas Marshall, James Ducat, and Donald MacArthur, standing next to the official who hired them, Robert Muirhead

A LONELY JOB

These days, the lighthouse is powered by electricity and works without needing a lighthouse keeper. But in the 19th century, lighthouse keepers had to spend weeks on the isolated island. There were four keepers—at any one time, three of them would manage the lighthouse, while one would be off-duty, back at home.

Eilean Mòr is only around 1600 ft. (500 m) long and less than 660 ft. (200 m) wide.

VANISHED!

On December 16, 1900, a passing ship noticed that the lighthouse was dark and raised the alarm. A relief boat was meant to visit the lighthouse to bring supplies and the fourth lighthouse keeper, but the weather was so stormy that it couldn't reach the island for another 10 days. When the boat finally arrived, things were not as they should be. Usually, boxes were left down by the landing stage (jetty) to be restocked, but they were nowhere to be found. When the boat's crew inspected the lighthouse, they found it deserted. There was no sign of the keepers anywhere on the island.

What was found at the lighthouse?

- The doors were locked.
- The oil lamps had been cleaned and filled—this was a job the keepers did every morning.
- Two sets of oilskins (waterproof outdoor clothing) were missing, but one set was still there—one of the three men must have gone outside without his oilskins.
- Outside, one of the island's landing stages had been badly damaged in the storms.

WHAT COULD HAVE HAPPENED?

FIGHT?

According to some people, one of the lighthouse keepers, Donald MacArthur, had a fiery temper. There were rumors that he may have started a fight near a cliff edge, ending with all three men falling into the treacherous sea. However, there is no evidence to back up this version of events.

RESCUE GONE WRONG?

It has also been suggested that, rather than fighting, two of the men may have died while trying to save the third, who had fallen into the sea. With wind and rain whipping the rugged coast, it would have been a dangerous place, even for these experienced lighthouse keepers.

SWEPT AWAY?

It seems most likely that the men were swept away by a giant wave. Perhaps two of the men went out during a powerful storm to save some equipment on the landing stage or the island's crane. The third lighthouse keeper, who was supposed to stay at the lighthouse no matter what, may have suddenly realized the peril his colleagues were in. Without putting on his oilskins, he may have rushed out to warn them, but was also swept away by the sea. This was certainly the view of Captain Harvie, the captain of the relief boat, who wrote: "A dreadful accident has happened at the Flannans… Poor fellows, they must have been blown over the cliffs or drowned trying to secure a crane."

This illustration shows the lighthouse's crane by the landing stage being used to lift a horse onto the island.

STILL A SECRET

Though there are different theories, we'll never know for sure what happened to the three lighthouse keepers. It's a secret that the island's windswept rocks are keeping to themselves.

THE LOCH NESS MONSTER

Something strange is said to lurk in the murky depths of Britain's largest lake… something big. With sightings going back hundreds of years, it's no wonder this Scottish cryptid is the most famous lake creature of all time. It is, of course, the Loch Ness Monster or, as it's affectionately come to be known, Nessie.

The monster is usually described as having a long neck, as in this early 20th-century illustration.

SEEING IS BELIEVING

As well as countless sightings in the loch, Nessie has also been seen on land several times. The first reported land sighting was in 1879, when a group of children spotted it "waddling" down the hillside toward the loch.

The vast lake is overlooked by the medieval ruins of Urquhart Castle.

A GOOD HIDING PLACE

Nessie's believers point out that Scotland's Loch Ness is a very good place to hide. It contains more water than any other lake in the United Kingdom and is very deep – 788 ft. (240 m) at its lowest point. The water is also extremely murky, which makes it difficult to see anything much that goes on below the surface.

THE "SURGEON'S PHOTOGRAPH"

Over the years, several photos claiming to be of Nessie have been taken. The most famous one, the "surgeon's photograph" (right), turned out to be a fake made from clay and a toy submarine.

NESSIE'S LAIR

Other evidence of Nessie includes this 1933 image, believed to be the first 'photo' of the creature. A huge underwater cavern has also been discovered in the loch, nicknamed Nessie's Lair. Is this where the monster hides? Furthermore, sonar exploration has shown large objects moving in the loch's depths. Could they be the legendary monster (or monsters)? Turn the page to find out more…

WHAT COULD IT BE?

For those who think they've caught a glimpse of Nessie, there is no question: there is some sort of huge creature lurking in the loch. But for those who doubt the lake monster is real, what could be another explanation for the sightings?

FLOATING OBJECTS?

Looking out across the vast Loch Ness, it's difficult to see distant objects clearly. Some Nessie sightings might actually be a floating log (right) or other debris. People may think it looks like the monster because the legend has already sparked their imagination.

GIANT EEL?

Scientists have suggested that some monster sightings could be giant eels. There are lots of European eels living in the loch, though they normally grow no longer than 4 ft. (1.3 m)—could one have become monster-sized? In the seas of the tropics, some moray eels (left) can be over 11 ft. (3.5 m) long, but they wouldn't survive in the loch's cold waters.

SWIMMING ELEPHANT?

One palaeontologist and Nessie researcher thinks that circus elephants may have gone for a dip in the loch in the 1930s, leading to mistaken monster sightings. These huge mammals might have been allowed to swim there for a refreshing break while traveling circuses were in the area.

THE BIG QUESTIONS

For many people, the answer to the mystery is obvious—Nessie is a monster, perhaps something that has survived from the time of the dinosaurs. Most sightings seem to match descriptions of extinct marine reptiles, such as Plesiosaurus (right). However, if Nessie is real, there are some big questions to answer…

- If Nessie has been around for millions of years, it's likely not the same individual. For the species to survive, there has to be more than one. Wouldn't that make them easier to spot or catch?
- With so many people searching for Nessie, and with modern cameras and smartphones, wouldn't someone have been able to get clear photographic evidence by now? Or has lots of practice just made Nessie good at hiding?
- Is there enough food for such a big creature in Loch Ness?

THE SEARCH CONTINUES

Despite the lack of hard evidence over the years, belief in Nessie remains strong. Scientists and tourists alike continue to scour the lake, hoping to be the one who captures a clear, unblurry photo and finally solves the mystery.

STONEHENGE

On Salisbury Plain in Wiltshire, South West England, a huge and ancient monument rises from the land. Though many of its stones have fallen, this incredible structure still conjures up a sense of magic and mystery. What could have driven its builders to create this prehistoric wonder?

What makes up Stonehenge?

- An outer ditch and bank of earth, dug around 3100 BCE
- An inner horseshoe and outer ring of massive, 23-ft (7-m) tall sandstone blocks (known as sarsen stones) with other stones sitting on top, built around 2500 BCE
- A ring of smaller stones, known as bluestones, from around 2300 BCE
- A large altar stone in the middle

MOVING STONES

Stonehenge's bluestones, which weigh between 2 and 5 tons, were brought all the way from Wales, around 180 miles (290 km) away, presumably rolled all the way. They must have been very important to the ancient peoples. The huge sarsen stones were transported from a quarry around 20 miles (32 km) from the site.

This was a much shorter journey, but with each stone weighing an eye-watering 22 tons, it must have taken incredible skill, strength, and determination to move them. But how this was achieved it is still a mystery.

Less than half of the original stones are still standing, as the photo (above) and plan (left) show.

LEGENDS

Over the centuries, different legends have tried to explain how Stonehenge came to be, including that the stones were brought there by the famous wizard Merlin, the Devil, or carried by giants.

WHAT WAS STONEHENGE USED FOR?

COSMIC CALENDAR?

The stone circle is positioned so that the Sun shines through the center at sunrise on the summer solstice (the longest day of the year) and at sunset on the winter solstice (the shortest day of the year). These times were important to the ancient Britons, perhaps because of their link to the changing seasons.

An early 19th-century illustration imagining what a religious ceremony at the ancient site may have looked like

RELIGIOUS CENTER?

It is thought that Stonehenge was a major religious center and that as many as 4,000 people might have come together each year to celebrate the summer and winter solstices. What form the ceremonies took, however, nobody knows.

SHRINE TO THE DEAD?

From the very beginning, Stonehenge was used as a burial site. It was likely seen as a very special and sacred place and might have been a place where ancestors were worshipped.

MYSTERY MONUMENT

In Stone Age Britain, 5,000 years ago, there was no such thing as reading and writing. All the information we have on Stonehenge is provided by its physical remains. With no written records, we may never know for sure how or why the ancient Britons managed to build such an impressive monument using only stone tools and wood. We may never know what ceremonies they performed there. What made Stonehenge such a special and sacred place may remain a mystery, forever lost in time.

EUROPE'S STANDING STONES

Though Stonehenge is the most famous of Europe's stone circles (page 70), there are many others scattered across the continent's landscape. Each is different, adding to the puzzling mystery of what ancient ceremonies were performed there.

THE DOLMEN OF GUADALPERAL, SPAIN

This stone circle, nicknamed the Spanish Stonehenge, disappeared beneath the waters created by a dam in 1963. Now, more than 60 years later, drought has dried up the waters, giving us a chance to glimpse this mysterious monument. It's thought to have been a temple and a burial site, built as far back as 5000 BCE. The stone circle has only been fully visible four times since it was first swallowed up by the dam water, and experts are worried that the watery conditions are damaging the stones. If nothing is done, the Dolmen may be lost forever.

THE RING OF BRODGAR, SCOTLAND

Standing tall against the wind and rain on the island of Orkney, these 4,000-year-old standing stones form an almost perfect circle. There were originally 60 towering stones, though only 36 remain. The Ring of Brodgar is one of the largest and most northerly stone circles in Britain, but archaeologists are unsure why it was built in this rugged, remote place. Some think it was a temple for religious rituals, while others think it was used to observe the movements of the Sun, Moon, and stars.

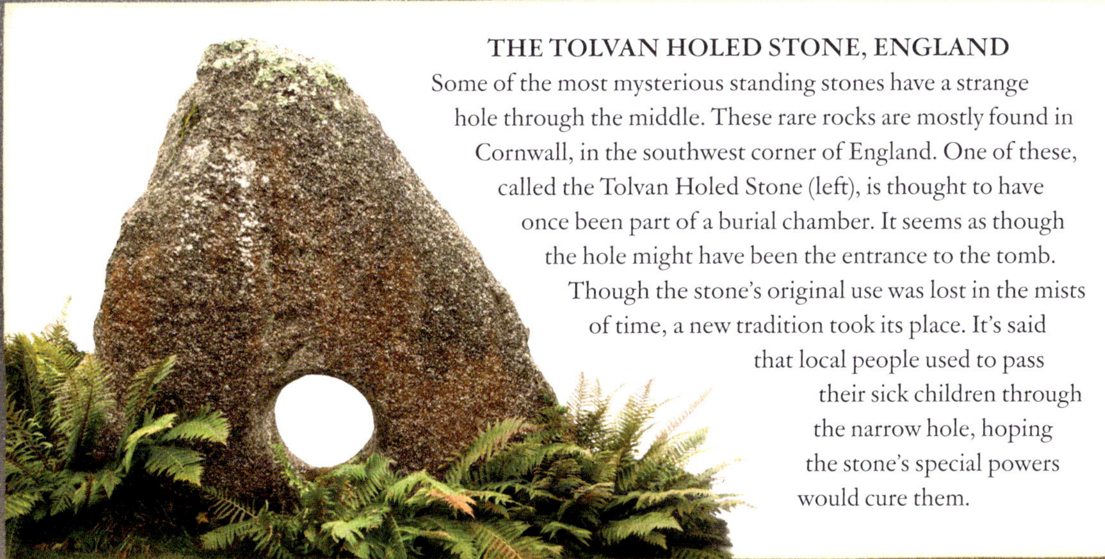

THE TOLVAN HOLED STONE, ENGLAND

Some of the most mysterious standing stones have a strange hole through the middle. These rare rocks are mostly found in Cornwall, in the southwest corner of England. One of these, called the Tolvan Holed Stone (left), is thought to have once been part of a burial chamber. It seems as though the hole might have been the entrance to the tomb. Though the stone's original use was lost in the mists of time, a new tradition took its place. It's said that local people used to pass their sick children through the narrow hole, hoping the stone's special powers would cure them.

PUNCHESTOWN LONGSTONE, IRELAND

Some mysterious stones have been positioned on their own. These are known as monoliths. One of these is the towering Punchestown Longstone, the tallest monolith in Ireland. At 23 ft. (7 m) high, it's nearly as tall as a two-story house. It's been carefully carved to be very smooth and slim. At its base is the site of a Bronze Age cremation burial.

THE CARNAC STONES, FRANCE

With more than 3,000 stones, the Carnac Stones in Brittany, France make up the largest monument of standing stones in the world. Many of the stones have been arranged in 11 long, straight rows, while others have been used to build burial chambers. Archaeologists think the stones were placed there around 6,000 years ago, but who built the monument and why is still shrouded in mystery. Many myths have tried to explain the stones —one says that they stand in such straight lines because they were once Roman soldiers who were turned to stone.

THE BEAST OF BODMIN MOOR

Here's a mystery to really sink your claws into. A huge black cat is said to be on the loose in South West England, prowling the wild and windswept Bodmin Moor. There have been dozens of sightings since 1978.

The police have been called out many times to reports of a big cat, and in 1995, the government even ordered an official investigation. It found no clear evidence that there was a cat out there... but it also didn't find any evidence against it.

What Does it Look Like?

A big black cat

- Like a puma or panther
- Long, thick tail
- Yellow shining eyes
- Around 3–5 ft. (1–1.5 m) long

Have you seen anything strange, perhaps a pair of glowing eyes, staring at you from the shadows?

Does this blurry picture taken in 2002 in Bodmin show a panther on the prowl?

CAUGHT ON CAMERA

Many photos have been taken that seem to show a big black cat, but the photos are often out of focus, and it's difficult to be sure of the animal's size. Could it just be a very big domestic cat?

BIG CATS EVERYWHERE

It's not just Bodmin Moor that is thought to be home to a mysterious beast. Since 2001, there have been big-cat sightings reported in 15 places across England, Scotland, and Wales.

WHAT COULD IT BE?

ESCAPED PUMAS?

In 1978, three pumas were meant to have been moved from Plymouth Zoo to Dartmouth Zoo in South West England, but supposedly never arrived. They were rumored to have been released on the moors, either accidentally or on purpose. Could they have bred in the wild, with descendants still living today? It's likely that, over the years, other big cats kept as exotic pets might have escaped or been abandoned too. However, experts say that there isn't enough food available on the moors for a family of big cats to live for generations. If they were eating farm animals, wouldn't many more of those animals have been killed or gone missing?

ANCIENT CATS?

Some people suggest that a handful of very rare big cats could have survived in the area from prehistoric times, back when Britain was a wild place with only a few human hunter-gatherers. Although wild animals like cave lions (above), bears, and lynx did live in Britain thousands of years ago, it seems unlikely that some big cats would have lived here all this time without leaving plenty of evidence.

A PLAIN OLD PUSSYCAT?

Sceptics claim that sightings of the Beast of Bodmin Moor are actually just people seeing a large pet cat but mistaking the distance. They think it is further away—and therefore larger—than it actually is. Maybe that is the case for some sightings, but a few of the photos of the Beast of Bodmin look pretty convincing...

THE TATZELWURM

As you breathe in the crisp air and gaze up at the snowcapped peaks of the Alps in central Europe, it's hard to imagine that such a beautiful mountain range could be home to a lizard-like monster with poisonous breath. Though it goes by many names, descriptions of this legendary creature are enough to send a chill down the spine of even the hardiest adventurer.

Beast of many names

Throughout history, the countries and regions around the Alps each had their own name for this menacing monster:

- Tatzelwurm (worm with claws) in parts of Germany and Austria
- Bergstutz (mountain-stump) in parts of Austria and Germany
- Stollenwurm (tunnel worm) in Switzerland
- Arassas (meaning unknown) in France

LIZARD CAT

The Tatzelwurm has been described as a kind of dragon with a lizard's body and a cat's head. It may have two, four, or six stubby legs, although in some accounts, the Tatzelwurm was described as being legless, more like some sort of serpent. Most accounts say the creature was black-gray in color, with scaly skin, but some reported it having fur. Over the centuries, descriptions of the monster's size have varied greatly, from around 1 ft. (30 cm) to a whopping 7 ft. (2 m) long.

BAD BREATH!

The Tatzelwurm's breath was said to be so poisonous that anyone smelling it would die. It also made an earsplitting shrieking or whistling sound, and it was even claimed in some reports that the monster could kill you just by looking at you!

WHAT COULD IT BE?

GILA MONSTER?

This large lizard has powerful claws and a venomous bite… but it is only found in parts of North America. It lives in deserts, not snowy mountains.

GIANT SALAMANDER?

Giant salamanders (below) can grow up to 5 ft. (1.5 m) long and have poisonous skin. However, they spend all their lives in rivers and streams. And furthermore, they live in East Asia and have never been found living in the wild in Europe.

OTTER?

These semiaquatic mammals have cat-like faces, long bodies, and stubby legs, and they do live in the Alps… but could these cute, small critters really be mistaken for a fearsome, serpent-like monster?

LONG GONE?

There are written accounts of people seeing the Tatzelwurm in the 17th, 18th, and 19th centuries, but since then the trail seems to have gone cold. Could there have once been some sort of weird creature roaming the Alps that is now extinct?

THE HAUNTED FOREST

Transylvania, a region in Romania, is famed for being the homeland of the legendary vampire Dracula. But it also lays claim to another creepy credential: it is there that you will find Hoia Baciu, said to be the world's most haunted forest.

WHAT'S WEIRD ABOUT HOIA BACIU?

Many of the trees grow in crooked, zigzag shapes, or clockwise spirals. Scientists haven't been able to explain why. Those who fear the twisted trees of Hoia-Baciu warn that it is the site of paranormal activity. When entering the woods, visitors have described experiencing everything from electronic devices that stop working to sightings of ghosts and UFOs.

SPOOKY STORIES

It is said that many people have wandered into this eerie hilltop forest, never to be seen again. This seems even more spooky, since the forest is tiny, covering an area of just 1 sq mile (3 sq km). One story tells of a five-year-old girl who was lost in the forest and then appeared again five years later, still the same age and wearing the same clothes. Another story claims that a shepherd went missing in the forest, along with his entire flock of 200 sheep.

PARANORMAL EFFECTS

People who visit the forest report feeling sick, anxious, and as though they are being watched. Some even claim to have suffered scratches and bruises but have no idea how they got them. Other are convinced they have seen ghosts—sometimes even photographing them. In 1968, a military technician called Emil Barnea photographed a shining silver disc hovering over part of the forest known as the Clearing (shown above in an artist's impression). He insisted it was a UFO and was fired from his job for making this bold claim.

THE CLEARING

The Clearing is a round area in the center of Hoia-Baciu. Could this be where UFOs land? It's' said that no living things grow here… except this doesn't seem to be true, as it's covered in grass, if not trees.

WHAT COULD IT BE?

With all the scary stories about Hoia-Baciu, you'll need to be especially brave to investigate the woods by day… and perhaps a little crazy to wander into them at night! But if you get past the fear factor, you might notice that there isn't much evidence to back up the rumors. Yes, it could be that ghosts and aliens call this tiny patch of forest home… or it could be people's imaginations running wild.

Things can look strange when we're scared. In the dark, this tree root in the forest could look like a giant claw.

SCARED SICK

People often report feelings of sickness, anxiety, and an eerie atmosphere when they visit the haunted forest. Could these feelings be real, but caused by their fear of the scary stories they have heard about Hoia-Baciu?

Maybe you'll need to visit Hoia-Baciu for yourself to decide if it deserves the title of World's Most Haunted Forest!

THE VOYNICH MANUSCRIPT

Is there anything more mysterious than an ancient book of secret writing that no one can read? There really is such a book. The Voynich manuscript is thought to be around 600 years old, but no one knows who wrote it or what its writings and drawings mean. Though many people have tried, not even the best code crackers can unravel its mystery.

THE BIZARRE BOOK

The mystery manuscript is a handwritten book made from calfskin parchment. It consists of over 200 pages of colorful drawings of people, unknown plants, and stars. Based on these illustrations, it's thought the manuscript includes a large section about herbs, as well as information on biology, medicine, astronomy, zodiac signs, and recipes. But exactly what this information is, no one knows.

MYSTERY ORIGINS

The mystery book has been named the Voynich manuscript after Wilfrid Voynich, the Polish book dealer who bought it in Italy in 1912 and brought it to international attention. However, the manuscript's ownership has been traced back to Emperor Rudolph II, the ruler of the Holy Roman Empire (a medieval European state), who bought it for 600 gold coins in around 1599. Researchers think before that it may have been owned by a botanist called Dr. Leonard Rauwolf who lived in what is now Germany.

UNCRACKABLE

Language scholars, expert code breakers and even the FBI have all reportedly failed to crack the manuscript's mysterious writing, which has been named "Voynichese."

Rudolph II clearly had a taste for the strange, as shown by his commissioning of this "fruit and vegetable" portrait by the Italian artist Giuseppe Arcimboldo.

WHAT COULD IT MEAN?

A HOAX?

Sceptics once suspected the manuscript was created by Wilfrid Voynich himself, who then pretended it was valuable and one-of-a-kind. But special tests, known as carbon dating, have shown that the manuscript was made in the early 1400s, so it couldn't be by Voynich. Some people have suggested that the manuscript—while made in medieval times—was still a hoax. They think that the text is meaningless nonsense, and that's why no one has been able to decipher it.

Voynich in his study

CLEVER CODE?

Some researchers think that the manuscript is in a European language, but that it's been written in a secret code using a made-up alphabet. Without knowing the code, it's very difficult to figure out what the words mean. If it is a code, it was presumably created by a learned scholar. Over the years, numerous names have been suggested for who this might be, including the 13th-century English philosopher Roger Bacon.

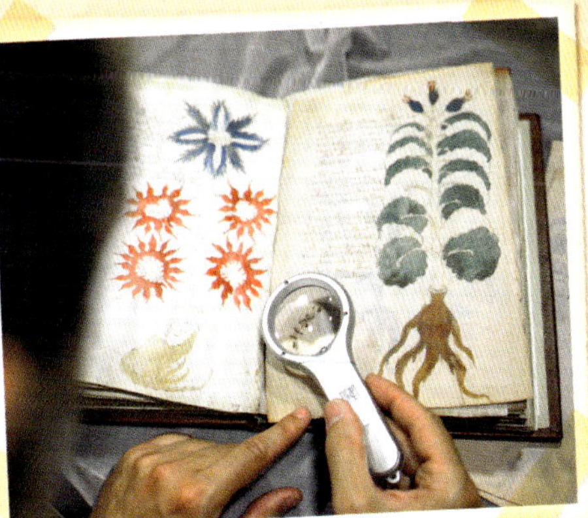

CRACKABLE AFTER ALL?

Following the huge breakthroughs in AI (artificial intelligence) in recent years, some scientists think it now might be possible to use computers to finally reveal the secrets of the mystery manuscript. However, there's no guarantee. Over the years, many scholars have claimed to have found the key to translating the Voynich manuscript, but so far all have been proven wrong. Will anyone unravel the world's most mysterious book? Perhaps you could be the one to finally unlock the answers...

THE ANTIKYTHERA MECHANISM

Off the coast of the Greek island of Antikythera, a shipwreck and its cargo lay hidden for more than 2,000 years until it was finally discovered by divers in 1900. In the sunken wreck, those divers found a puzzling bronze object. Though it was badly damaged by the saltwater, it was clear that this mysterious artifact was unlike anything found before. It appeared to be some sort of ancient computer... but surely that was impossible!

WHAT IS IT?

Now known as the Antikythera Mechanism, this shoebox-sized instrument was built sometime between 200 and 60 BCE. It has been nicknamed a "clockwork computer" because it works in a similar way to a clock, but with at least 30 gearwheels inside, some of which can be seen in this photo of the artifact. It also had seven hands —many more than the two or three on a clock used to tell the time! Amazingly, it is far more complex than anything else made at the time, or even for another thousand years.

Like these ancient Greek pottery shards, the wreck and mechanism were found lying on the seabed.

WHAT WAS IT USED FOR?

Experts think that the device might have been used to teach astronomy. It's thought that its dials were turned to predict the movement of the Sun, Moon, and planets and the timing of astronomical events such as eclipses (right).

SPACECRAFT TECH?

Though most people agree that a skilled ancient Greek craftsman likely made the fascinating "clockwork computer," some people have speculated that something so ahead of its time must have been made by aliens!

UNLOCKING SECRETS

For years, the mysterious artifact sat in a museum, but no one understood much about what it was for. It wasn't until more than 70 years after the Antikythera Mechanism was found that scientists could finally learn more about it using X-rays to look past its badly damaged surface. In 2006, even more details were revealed by CT scans, and scientists were able to reconstruct what the mechanism may have looked like.

This reconstruction shows that the mechanism had several arms that could show the timings of events, including festivals.

ROMAN DODECAHEDRONS

While the Antikythera Mechanism is one of a kind, there is a type of mysterious ancient object that has been found dotted across France and other parts of Europe: Roman dodecahedrons (below). These 12-sided hollow bronze objects have perplexed archaeologists for years. What they were used for is a complete mystery, and no mention of them has been found in any writing from the time.

So far, more than 100 dodecahedrons have been uncovered. Most of them are about the size of a clenched fist and they were made in the second and third centuries CE. It's likely that they were valuable to their Roman owners, since some have been found in hoards of coins, which were buried to keep them hidden and safe.

It's been suggested that the strange objects could have been some kind of military tool or a measuring device, a religious or magical item, a calendar, a fortune-telling device, or even a tool for knitting gloves—after all, it's only been found in places that get pretty chilly in winter!

HAUNTED EUROPE

With its long, often bloodthirsty history, Europe has no shortage of ghost stories and tales of mysterious goings on. Here are just a handful of the most haunted locations...

ZVIKOV CASTLE, CZECH REPUBLIC

An ancient supernatural being is fabled to haunt the castle's Black Tower (the square tower in the center of this photo). Seen as an evil imp or trickster, it has made the castle its home for hundreds of years. It is still said to get up to mischief, tripping up visitors, blowing out flames, and making electronic equipment stop working. If that doesn't sound too scary, legend has it that anyone who sleeps in the tower will die within the year.

MALAHIDE CASTLE, IRELAND

This 800-year-old castle near Dublin in Ireland (above) is said to be home to at least five ghosts. These include a mysterious 'Lady in White' who steps out of her portrait to roam the many rooms. One of the castle's more gruesome ghosts is said to be the spirit of Miles Corbett, a man who was given the castle by the English ruler Oliver Cromwell in 1649. Corbett was later brutally hanged, drawn, and quartered as punishment for the part he played in the execution of King Charles I. People have reported seeing his ghost running through the castle on the anniversary of his death.

THE BLOODY SQUARE, SWEDEN

Stockholm's grand square, Stortorget, has a grizzly history. It was there in November 1520 that the invading Danish King Kristian II executed 92 Swedish noblemen. People reported that there was so much blood that it flooded the square and stayed there for months. To this day, it is reported that in November, by moonlight, blood can be seen on the ground. Yet, spookily, if you try to touch the ghostly liquid, it disappears.

THE COLOSSEUM, ITALY

When the Roman Colosseum (left) was built 2,000 years ago, it was used for gladiator battles, chariot races and even public executions. With such a gruesome history, it's no surprise that people report seeing ghosts. A long-dead Roman soldier is often spotted guarding the Colosseum at night, while visitors also claim to hear screams of pain echoing across the amphitheater. The chilling wails are thought to come from the many unfortunate people who were killed in front of the cheering crowds.

PARIS CATACOMBS, FRANCE

Walk down a spiral staircase and you'll find one of the most eerie places in Europe. Deep under the streets of Paris are the Catacombs (right)—creepy chambers holding millions of human bones and skulls, all neatly on display! The catacombs were built to hold the human remains when there was no room left in Paris's cemeteries in the 18th and 19th centuries. Legend has it that scary voices can be heard coming from the walls after midnight. The voices will try to get you to walk farther into the maze of tombs, until you are lost forever.

THE CROOKED FOREST

In a forest in Poland there is an otherworldly glade. Step into it and you might feel as if you've entered a strange parallel universe, where everything is just a bit different… for here 400 pine trees grow in bizarre shapes that don't seem to conform to the rules of nature. This is the mysterious Crooked Forest.

STRANGE PHENOMENON

The crooked trees are thought to have been planted in around 1930. Their trunks bend outward, close to the ground, forming a shape like the letter *J*. Incredibly, they have all grown in exactly the same shape and are pointing in the same northward direction. The grove is surrounded by a pine forest where the trees are all normal.

No one is sure what happened to the trees to make them grow in such a bizarre way.

DANCING FOREST

A similar forest can be found in Russia. Here, the trunks of the pine trees are twisted into a variety of shapes, including spirals, hearts, and rings.

WHAT COULD HAVE HAPPENED?

SNOWED UNDER?

One theory about how the trees grew crooked is that they were bent under a thick layer of snow when they were young saplings.

WEIRD GRAVITY?

One very sci-fi suggestion is that the tree trunks may have been affected by a strange gravitational pull in that area. If so, it's one that has been observed nowhere else on Earth.

HUMAN-MADE?

A third theory is that the tree trunks' shape is not natural, but human-made. It is thought that the foresters who planted the grove may have bent the young trees on purpose. They might have done this to try to produce curved wood, useful for boatbuilding or making furniture. If so, the trees were probably abandoned when the Second World War broke out in 1939. Experts think this is the most likely explanation.

FUNGUS?

Another suggestion is that the trees were affected by a fungus when they were saplings, which might have made them grow crooked. Although there is a fungus known to affect pine trees, it's never had such an extreme effect on other trees.

ALIENS?

Some UFO enthusiasts have suggested the bizarre forest might be the work of extraterrestrials, but there is no evidence this is true… or why an alien would want to bend a few trees! But if aliens do exist, would we understand how their minds work? Maybe it's a message—or a sign that we just haven't figured out yet.

THE BLUE GROTTO

The island of Capri, Italy, has an enchanting spectacle… but you'll have to wait until low tide to see it. Tucked away on the coast is a very unusual sea cave known as the Blue Grotto. Those who are lucky enough to get inside this strange cavern are captivated by a world of shimmering blue light. For centuries, visitors couldn't understand where the light came from.

FIT FOR AN EMPEROR

The Blue Grotto is so spectacular that the Roman Emperor Tiberius used to swim in it 2,000 years ago. He had the grotto decorated with statues of Neptune and Triton, gods of the sea. It's thought that more statues may still be lying on the cave floor below the waves.

The inside of the cave glitters with a shimmering blue light.

THE CURSED CAVE

After Tiberius's time, the cave became known as a place of evil spirits. The people of Capri thought it was home to witches, devils, and monsters. For centuries, sailors avoided getting too close. According to legend, in the 1600s, a couple of priests finally plucked up the courage to enter the cave. But, upon seeing the Roman statues and ghostly blue light, they turned and fled.

WHAT CAUSES THE LIGHT?

In reality, there is a natural reason for the blue light. There is a large hole in the cave's side, deep underwater below the small entrance. Light from the outside enters the cave from this hole, but the water stops the red parts of the light from getting through, leaving only the blue color. The grotto's water is very clear, allowing the blue light to fill the space.

Today, the grotto is a major tourist attraction. In summer, boats line up, waiting to enter.

CROP CIRCLES

If you walked through a cornfield and came across a strange area of flattened stalks, you might not be able to figure out what you were looking at. But look down from an airplane and you'll see the whole picture: a mysterious pattern pressed into the crops.

MYSTERY MARKINGS

There are records of strange markings in fields over the centuries, but the first of what we now think of as crop circles was found in Wiltshire, England, in 1978. The discovery caused a flurry of excitement in the media, and many more circles sprang up across southern England over the next decade. With the patterns seeming to appear overnight and out of nowhere, many people guessed they were UFO landing sights.

SOLVED

IT'S A HOAX

In 1991, pranksters Doug Bower and Dave Chorley admitted that they had made the 1978 crop circle and more than 200 others since then. They claimed to have used a simple plank of wood and a length of rope to create the huge patterns.

THE CRAZE CONTINUES

While we now know that people are responsible for the otherworldly patterns, that hasn't stopped the craze. In fact, they seem to be getting larger and more complex than ever. In the years since Bower and Chorley's first crop circle, thousands more have appeared across the world. Drones are now used to film the incredible artworks from the air, and visitors flock to new crop circles to see them with their own eyes. If an alien looked down from a spaceship, perhaps it would be just as impressed!

MYSTERIOUS SEAS

KEY

Our oceans and seas hold many secrets. While tales of monstrous sea serpents, terrifying ghost ships, and the notorious Bermuda Triangle have kept many travelers on dry land, others have searched the endless blue in hopes of finding the Lost City of Atlantis or a glimpse of a mermaid.

THE BERMUDA TRIANGLE

For decades, an area of the Atlantic Ocean has had a reputation for mysterious disappearances, where ships and planes seem to vanish without a trace. If you listen to some people, the Bermuda Triangle is a paranormal zone you'd have to be crazy to travel through. To others, it is nothing more than an urban legend. What do you think?

What is the Bermuda Triangle?

- An area of sea roughly between the tip of Florida and the islands of Bermuda and Puerto Rico
- Covers around 500,000 square miles (1.3 million sq km) of ocean
- First described in 1952, and first named the Bermuda Triangle in 1964
- Also nicknamed the Devil's Triangle

Bermuda

Miami

Puerto Rico

COLUMBUS'S COMPASS

There were signs of something strange going on in the Bermuda Triangle long before it got its name. In 1492, the famous Italian explorer Christopher Columbus noted in his ship's log that his compass wasn't pointing north as it should. He kept it a secret from his crew so as not to cause panic. Just a few days later, he noticed a peculiar light, far out at sea.

USS *CYCLOPS*

Many ships and aircraft have met a sticky end while traveling across this notorious area of ocean. In 1918, the navy ship USS *Cyclops* and its 306-strong crew went missing without a trace after leaving Barbados. Possible explanations put forward at the time included being sunk in a storm, structural failure, or being overloaded with a heavy cargo.

The USS *Cyclops* photographed in 1911

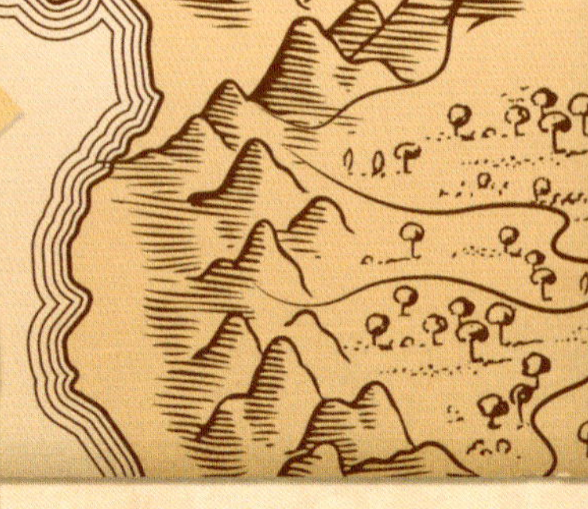

FLIGHT 19

Flight 19 was a US Navy training flight that included five torpedo bomber planes. All five vanished while flying over the Atlantic Ocean in 1945. Before they disappeared, the lead pilot radioed the base to say their compasses weren't working and they were lost. Adding to the intrigue, a plane that was sent out to search for the missing squadron also disappeared. It is thought to have exploded in midair.

A group of five bomber planes similar to the one that mysteriously disappeared

Was faulty equipment and human error to blame, or some strange phenomenon that affected the region's magnetic fields? The US Navy's theory was that the pilots had probably made a mistake in their navigation, then ran out of fuel before they reached land, crashing into the ocean. Whatever the cause, the squadron's mysterious disappearance sparked great interest in what was to become known as the Bermuda Triangle.

LOST PASSENGER FLIGHT

In 1948, a Douglas DC-3 aircraft carrying 29 passengers and 3 crew vanished while flying from Puerto Rico to Florida. Despite being investigated, no trace of the aircraft was found, and no reason for its likely crash was discovered. To this day, its disappearance remains a complete mystery.

A Douglas DC-3 similar to the one that vanished in 1948

WITCHCRAFT

In 1967, the captain of a small boat called *Witchcraft* reported that his vessel had hit something underwater and would need to be towed back to shore. But when the coast guard reached the spot a short time later, *Witchcraft* was gone. A large area of ocean was searched, but the boat and its two occupants were never seen again.

Turn the page to find out what might have caused the disappearances…

WHAT COULD HAVE CAUSED THE DISAPPEARANCES?

The Bermuda Triangle has captured imaginations around the world. People have come up with both natural and supernatural explanations to try to solve the mystery.

STORMS?

When a big storm hits, the ocean can quickly become deadly. The Bermuda Triangle is known to experience a particularly large number of hurricanes, which could be responsible for some of the disappearances.

CURRENTS AND WHIRLPOOLS?

The Bermuda Triangle has several strong currents, which can catch a ship off guard, pushing it off course. In places where currents meet, whirlpools can form. There are many sailing legends about giant whirlpools dragging ships down to the bottom of the sea. However, most whirlpools are too small to damage a ship, and they tend to form in known places, such as the one on the left in the Naruto Strait off the coast of Japan—but could there be some undiscovered ones out there?

METHANE GAS BUBBLES?

One theory for some mysterious sinkings is that methane that has collected under the ocean floor can sometimes burst upward, creating areas of frothy, bubbly water that can no longer hold up the weight of a ship. If these explosions happened in the Bermuda Triangle, they might have caused ships to suddenly sink. This is thought to be the fate of a fishing boat that sank near Scotland. It was otherwise undamaged when it sank to the bottom of an area known to give off gas bubbles, called Witch's Hole. Could something similar be happening in the Bermuda Triangle?

These methane gas bubbles are trapped in a frozen lake. In warmer waters, the bubbles are invisible—and possibly deadly.

TIME WARPS?

One of the wackier explanations is that there is some sort of time warp or gateway to a parallel universe in the Bermuda Triangle. Some stories tell of ships or planes that have seemingly "lost" time while in the Triangle, though there is no reliable evidence that this is true.

MAGNETIC FIELDS?

It's often claimed that weird magnetic fields are present in this part of the ocean, which can interfere with how planes and ships operate, causing instruments to go haywire. Although problems with compasses have been reported, there are no known irregularities caused by the magnetic fields around the Triangle. But there is much about the Earth's magnetic field that we still don't understand.

ALIENS?

There may not be any evidence that extra-terrestrials are behind the unexplained disappearances, but some UFOlogists think it's still a definite possibility! Many of the missing planes seemed to disappear in midair as if snatched away by an unseen presence. Could aliens be removing craft, perhaps to study them? And could that explain why no wreckage has been found of most of the disappeared ships and planes?

DEEP-SEA TRENCHES?

Believers in paranormal explanations often point to the lack of wreckage as proof that something mysterious has taken place. But it can often be difficult to track down wreckage in the vastness of the ocean. It can be especially tricky in the Bermuda Triangle, as there are some incredibly deep trenches that wrecks may have drifted into, making it very unlikely that a search party could ever find them. In fact, the Triangle is home to the deepest point in the Atlantic, at 5.2 miles (8.38 km) below sea level!

WEIRD NATURE

Sceptics argue that there have not been more disappearances or accidents in the Bermuda Triangle than elsewhere in the world oceans, and that reports of the numbers of vessels disappearing have been exaggerated. Others maintain that there is definitely something spooky and unexplained going on. Whatever the truth, it's clear that the world's oceans still hold so many mysteries for us to uncover.

THE MYSTERY OF THE MERMAID

For hundreds of years, there have been stories of merpeople living in the seas. In some legends, these half-fish, half-humans are beautiful and kind. Other stories warn of quick, fierce creatures who trick sailors, luring them into danger. Most think these magical figures are simply a myth, but in 2009, there was a very strange sighting that changed some people's minds.

SUNSET SIGHTINGS

The curious sighting happened at the seaside town of Kiryat Yam in Israel and the Palestinian Territories. Local people claimed they saw a mermaid: a girl with the tail of a dolphin. She was said to appear only at sunset and had been seen lying on the sand before disappearing into the ocean.

FLOCKS OF TOURISTS

Excitement about this incredible discovery spread, attracting many visitors eager to get a glimpse of the so-called mermaid for themselves. Although there were reports of sightings for many months, no one managed to take a clear photo or video of the mysterious fish-girl.

A $1 million reward was offered by the local government to the first person to photograph the mermaid. In 2013, two men claimed to have taken footage of the creature. However, they were not awarded the prize, and there have been suggestions that the images were faked.

A 19th-century fake mermaid

FAKE MERMAIDS

This wasn't the first time that people became convinced mermaids really existed. In the 1800s, sailors brought back strange, dried-up specimens said to be mermaids. It turned out they were actually the tail end of a fish sewn to the head and body of a monkey. They were fakes made and sold by fishermen in Japan.

WHAT COULD IT BE?

A HOAX?

Perhaps the mermaid sighting was nothing more than a hoax or prank. It is possible to buy mermaid tail costumes, so maybe the "mermaid" was just a person wearing one of these on the beach, hoping to fool whoever was looking.

In medieval times, sailors sometimes mistook marine mammals, such as seals and manatees, for mermaids.

A SEA CREATURE?

From a distance, it can sometimes be difficult to tell exactly what you are looking at. Perhaps the mermaid was actually a seal seen slipping into the water. Seals are rarely spotted on Israel's shores, so it would be understandable if people didn't immediately recognize what they were seeing. And, once the mermaid rumor began, other people might have become convinced they had spotted something unusual too.

A TRICK OF THE LIGHT?

Sightings of the mermaid happened at sunset, when the Sun was low and shadows were long. Perhaps this lighting made people think they saw something strange, and their imagination ran wild.

A MERMAID?

Some people believe they really saw a mermaid basking on the coast. Legends of merpeople are common in cultures across the world. Could there be something behind them? After all, it's exciting to think there might still be something magical out there waiting to be discovered.

ATLANTIS

For thousands of years, the legend of the Lost City of Atlantis has captivated mystery-seekers. Was there ever really such a place? Could a whole civilisation have sunk beneath the waves without a trace? And what riches might await any diver who finds this watery wonder?

A TALL TALE?

Plato claimed that this lost city existed 9,000 years before his own lifetime, and that the story had been passed down through the generations. However, we only have Plato's word for it. Could he have been making the whole thing up?

PLATO'S STORY

In around 360 BCE, the Greek philosopher Plato (left) wrote about Atlantis, an incredible land made out of rings of islands and canals with a grand city at its center. According to the legend, Atlantis was founded by rulers who were half-god, half-human, and the land contained great riches and wonderful wildlife. But, so the story goes, Atlantis was tragically destroyed, vanishing beneath the waves.

This artist's impression shows a lucky diver discovering the remains of Atlantis. While most scientists think that Atlantis is just a myth, some say that the story could have been based on a real city that was destroyed by a tsunami or volcanic eruption.

OCEAN MAPPING

Today, oceanographers are able to use sonar to produce images of the ocean floor, such as this one. So far, no trace of an ancient sunken city has been found, but there is still a lot of the ocean that hasn't been checked.

WHERE COULD THE LOST CITY BE?

ALMOST ANYWHERE?

Atlantis believers have tried to track down evidence of where the fabled sunken city might be. It has been claimed that Atlantis was in the Mediterranean Sea, the Canary Islands or the Azores in the Atlantic Ocean, off the coast of North America, and even Antarctica! So far, no one has found any concrete evidence.

SANTORINI?

Many people think that the “real” Atlantis may have been on the Greek island of Santorini (below), once known as Thera. The whole area in the center of the island, now covered by sea, was destroyed by an enormous volcanic eruption in 1600 BCE. This wiped out the Minoan town of Akrotiri and tsunami waves may have devastated other coastal towns, possibly playing a part in the collapse of the Minoan civilisation.

An artist’s impression of the flooding of an ancient civilisation

THE BLACK SEA?

Some believe that the story of Atlantis was inspired by the flooding of the Black Sea. Around 5500 BCE, the Black Sea was a freshwater lake, half its current size. The rising Mediterranean Sea rushed in, flooding the whole area with saltwater, destroying the settlements along the lake’s shore.

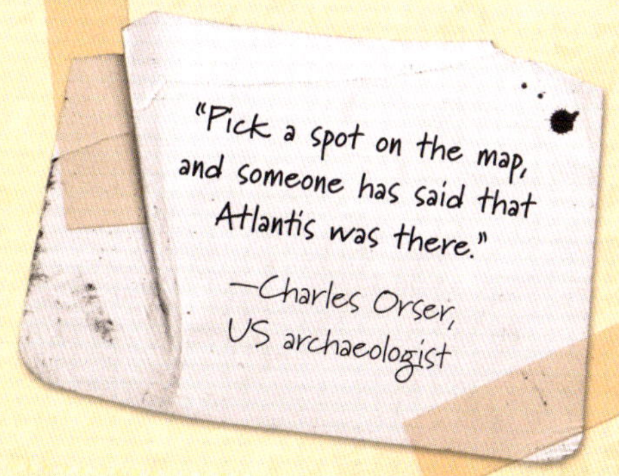

SPANISH WETLANDS?

Some researchers have claimed that satellite images show the ruins of Atlantis in wetlands off the southern coast of Spain. However, most archaeologists think the ruins are Greek or Roman. But until its location is proved (or its existence finally disproved), the speculation will continue.

THE *MARY CELESTE*

Imagine you are on a ship far out at sea in the vast Atlantic Ocean when another vessel appears on the horizon. As you come closer, you spot that it is drifting aimlessly, and its sails are damaged. You board this eerie ship and call out, but there is no answer. Everyone has disappeared. What happened to the crew of the *Mary Celeste*, a trading ship traveling from New York to Italy, remains a mystery to this day. There have been many theories—which do you think is the most likely?

Timeline of the disappearance

November 7, 1872: The *Mary Celeste* sets sail. There are 10 people on board, including the crew, Captain Benjamin Briggs, his wife, and their two-year-old daughter.

November 25: Early in the morning, after 18 days at sea, the captain writes his last entry in the ship's logbook.

December 4: The deserted *Mary Celeste* is spotted drifting near the Azores islands by the crew of another ship, the *Dei Gratia*.

The lifeboat is gone, along with some of the ship's papers, but there are no signs of a struggle.

December 13: The *Mary Celeste* arrives in Europe, sailed there by some of the *Dei Gratia*'s crew. Soon, the mystery of the ship spreads around the world. Numerous theories are put forward.

WHAT COULD HAVE HAPPENED?

PIRATES?

It seems unlikely that the *Mary Celeste* was boarded by pirates. There were no signs of blood or a struggle, and none of the cargo or other valuables were taken.

CONSPIRACY?

An inquiry was held to try to figure out what had happened to the ship. There were suspicions that the captain and crew of the *Dei Gratia* may have got rid of the crew of the *Mary Celeste* in order to "save" the ship and claim the salvage reward. Nothing was ever proven.

PANIC?

When it was found, the *Mary Celeste* had around 3 ft. (1 m) of water sloshing around in its hold. That shouldn't have been enough to put it danger, but perhaps the captain panicked. He may have thought it would be better for the crew to take the lifeboat and row to land. However, the captain was experienced and it was thought unlikely that he would have made such a rash decision. Had some other catastrophe struck the ship?

GIANT SEA CREATURE?

At the time, there were stories that a huge sea monster could have reached out of the water and devoured the crew. But if that were the case, wouldn't the ship have been wrecked?

A 19th-century painting of a sea monster about to attack a sailing ship

WAS THE SHIP CURSED?

When the *Mary Celeste* was built in 1861, it was named *Amazon*. After being badly damaged in a storm six years later, the ship was sold as a wreck. It was restored by its new owner, who also gave it a new name. However, renaming a ship is considered bad luck… could it be that from this moment on, the *Mary Celeste* was cursed?

THE *FLYING DUTCHMAN*

Crashing waves and howling winds can make the ocean a scary place, even in a modern ship. So, can you imagine how terrifying it would be to look out across the horizon and spot the eerie glow of a ghost ship gliding toward you? Legend has it that the *Flying Dutchman* signals doom to any sailor unfortunate enough to glimpse it.

THE LEGEND BEGINS

Different versions of the *Flying Dutchman* ghost ship story have been told over the centuries. The most famous tale dates from the late 18th century and begins with a trading vessel making its way back to the Netherlands from the Far East loaded with riches. Everyone on board is looking forward to getting home and sharing the bounty. But as the ship approaches the treacherous Cape of Good Hope on the coast of South Africa, a terrible storm erupts.

Despite the ferocity of the winds, the ship's captain, Hendrick van der Decken, refuses to change course and head for safety. Instead, he shouts out that he is determined to succeed even if he has to keep sailing for eternity. The Devil apparently hears his oath and decides to hold the captain to his word, condemning him and his ship to endlessly sail the oceans, doomed never to rest again.

Sightings

Over the years, there have been many reported sightings of the phantom ship:

- In 1881, near the South African coast, it was witnessed by none other than a teenage prince, the future King George V of Britain.
- During the Second World War, German U-boat (submarine) crews claimed to have seen the ghostly vessel in a similar location.
- In 1923, an officer and three other witnesses on a British steamship reported seeing a luminous sailing ship glowing, which disappeared as it was coming toward them.
- There are countless other similar stories of the ghostly apparition. In some, witnesses have reported hearing a party on board the phantom ship, with laughter, music, and lights.

Scene from an opera based on the ship

SCIENTIFIC EXPLANATION?

While superstitious sailors may live in dread of encountering the doom-laden *Flying Dutchma*n, scientists have come up with another—but still fascinating—explanation. The ghostly sightings could be caused by an optical illusion called a Fata Morgana. This happens when the atmosphere has just the right conditions for a ship to be reflected in the sky, forming a larger, image floating above the horizon, as in the photo on the right.

THE YONAGUNI MONUMENT

Beneath the waves of the Pacific Ocean, a strange "monument" has sparked debate. Is it a natural rock formation that just happens to look human-made… or is it actually the ruins of an ancient city, sunk by a catastrophic earthquake? First discovered in 1986, the intriguing underwater site lies off the coast of Yonaguni, a Japanese island close to Taiwan.

What lies beneath the waves?

- A collection of large stone structures on the seabed
- The biggest looks like a stepped pyramid and is more than 165 ft. (50 m) long and 65 ft. (20 m) wide.
- There are other rock structures on the surrounding seabed, covering an area around 1,000 ft. (300 m) by 500 ft. (150 m).
- Some of the rocks have carved lines on them that look like drawings.

The structure's straight faces and sharp angles certainly look human-made.

WHAT COULD IT BE?

A JAPANESE ATLANTIS?

A geologist called Masaaki Kimura, who was one of the first people to study the rocks, is convinced that they are human-made. He has suggested that the 'monument' could be thousands of years old, and includes ruins of a pyramid, a castle, temples, and roads, as well as carvings of animals. Kimura believes that the land shifted during an earthquake, pulling the ancient city beneath the waves.

Kihachiro Aratake, the operator of a diving company, discovered the monument while looking for somewhere to observe sharks.

An artist's impression showing Mu as a highly advanced civilisation before its destruction

A LOST CONTINENT?

Mu, also known as Lemuria, is a mythical Pacific continent said to have vanished beneath the waves, much like the legendary Atlantis (page 98). Its existence was first suggested by an archaeologist in the 19th century but, today, scientists insist that it's not possible for a whole continent to have simply sunk beneath the ocean. However, a city might have. Perhaps the tale of the continent was just exaggeration and there's a kernel of truth to the legend.

NATURAL WONDER?

Kimura's idea of sunken ruins from a lost civilisation are exciting, but most geologists who have visited the site disagree with him. They think the strange structures can be explained by natural forces acting on the sandstone rocks. They argue that earthquakes are known to split rocks in the way seen at Yonaguni and that strong currents wear away the stone. Scientists also report that the "monument" is made of the same solid rock that forms the seabed, rather than separate individual blocks placed on top of it.

A 3D map of the site

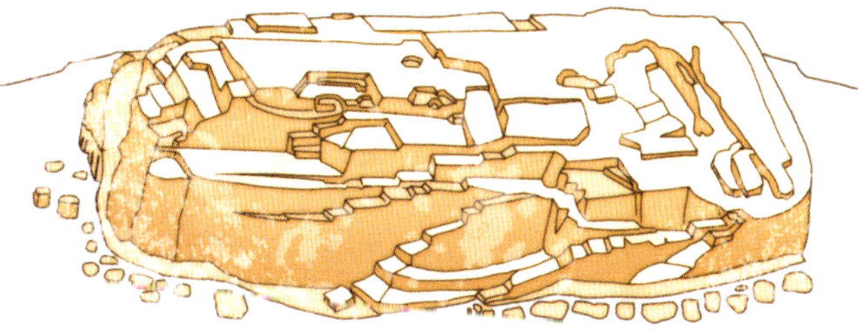

A MIX OF BOTH

It's been suggested that while most of the 'monument' is likely a natural rock formation, some of it could have been worked on by humans, chiseling steps or carving lines into the stone. Experts think the area flooded 10,000 years ago, so this would mean a very ancient culture lived nearby. As scientists continue to study the site, they are sure to uncover more answers. Until then, the Yonaguni Monument remains a popular diving spot for those who want to see the strange underwater structures for themselves.

AMELIA EARHART

Flying pioneer Amelia Earhart was famous across the world for her record-breaking solo flights. Though she knew the dangers involved, the thrill of flying always spurred her on to her next adventure. But while attempting to become the first woman to fly around the globe, Earhart vanished without a trace...

RECORD BREAKER

Born in 1897, Amelia gained her pilot license in 1923, one of the first women to do so. Less than 10 years later, in 1932, she achieved the incredible feat of becoming the first woman to fly solo across the Atlantic Ocean—and in record time. In 1935, she would go on to set another record, becoming the first person to fly solo from Hawaii to California.

TRIP OF A LIFETIME

On June 1, 1937, Amelia set off on what would be her final challenge. She aimed to fly around the world with her navigator, Fred Noonan. Starting from Oakland, and heading east, the journey was to take over a month and cover 29,000 miles (47,000 km). They would need to land their small plane many times along the way in order to refuel.

DISASTER

Having successfully flown more than halfway around the world, Amelia and Fred took off from Lae, an island in New Guinea, on July 2. They were heading for the tiny and remote Howland Island, 2,600 miles (4,200 km) away. The weather was cloudy, making it difficult to navigate. That evening, they radioed to say they were struggling to find Howland Island. Soon after, all contact was lost. Amelia, Fred, and their airplane had disappeared without a trace.

Earhart standing next to the plane in which she disappeared

THE SEARCH

A huge search party was sent out. Several ships and dozens of aircraft combed the seas and islands looking for any signs of Earhart and Noonan, but found nothing. Amelia and Fred were gone. Finally, Amelia was declared dead on January 5, 1939, two and a half years after the tragic accident.

WHAT COULD HAVE HAPPENED?

Earhart's daring adventures inspired the world, and the mystery of her disappearance continues to capture imaginations. There are many theories about what happened on her final flight…

SECRET MISSION?

There have been some rather wild conspiracy theories over the years, including that Amelia Earhart became a spy for the US government, was captured by the Japanese, or secretly went back to America and changed her name! However, there's no evidence that any of these are true. In 2017, a US TV documentary claimed to have uncovered a picture taken in 1937 proving that Earhart and Noonan had been captured by the Japanese. It showed two European figures, a man and a woman, in the Marshall Islands, then occupied by Japan. But subsequent research has shown that the photo was taken in 1935 and did not show the two aviators.

The documentary claimed the circled figures were Earhart and Noonan.

ISLAND LANDING?

Some people think Amelia and Fred could have flown off course and landed close to the Pacific island of Nikumaroro. It's been claimed that a piece of aluminum that matched part of Earhart's plane was found on the island, as well as a shoe and some bones. If these really did belong to Amelia, it may mean that she managed to swim to shore, but later died on the island.

CRASHED AT SEA?

Though we may never know for sure what happened to the pioneering pilot, the most likely answer is that Amelia and Fred were unable to find the island they had been hoping to land on and their plane ran out of fuel, plunging into the Pacific Ocean. In 2024, a pair of US explorers claimed to have located what may be the wreckage of a plane on the seabed near Howland Island, around 3 miles (5 km) down. But their sonar pictures are inconclusive. Until the wreckage is positively identified, people will continue to put forward other possible explanations.

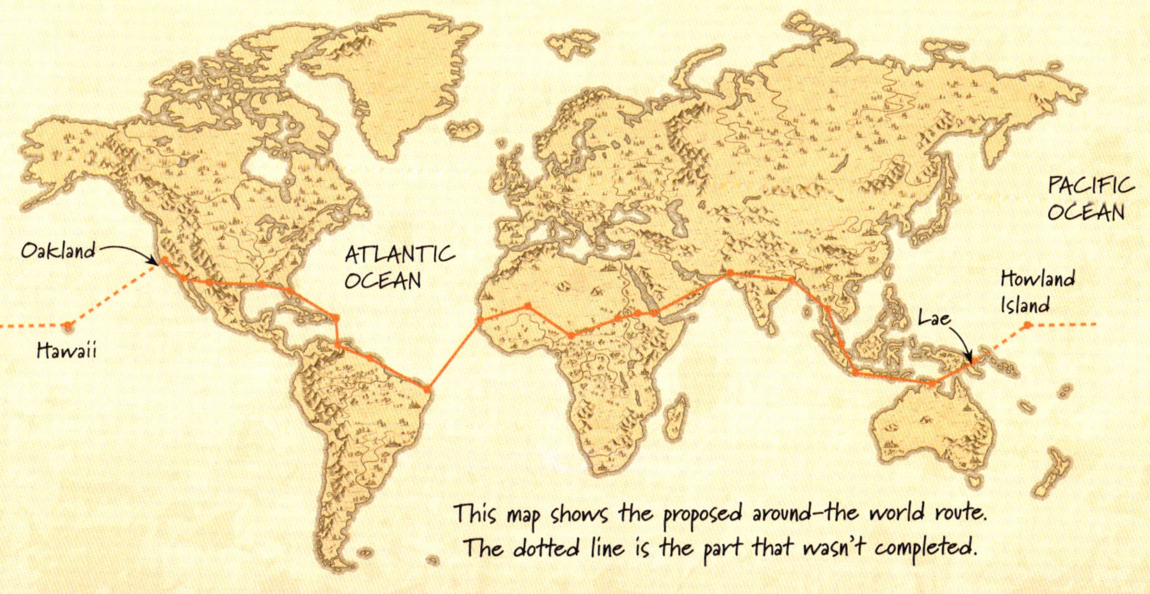

This map shows the proposed around-the world route. The dotted line is the part that wasn't completed.

THE KRAKEN

For hundreds of years, sailors have told of gigantic sea monsters lurking in the ocean's depths, ready to gobble up unsuspecting ships and pull them down into a salty grave. One monster is more famous—and feared—than any other: the enormous, squid-like Kraken. But could there be a grain of truth behind this tale? After all, it's been said that we know more about the surface of the Moon than we do about the deepest depths of the ocean...

THE KING'S MONSTER

The legend of the Kraken can be traced back to an account written in 1180 by Sverre, the then King of Norway. According to the monarch, the Kraken was a colossal beast, as large as an island. It was able to sink ships and was said to live in the seas around Norway, Iceland, and Greenland.

WORLDWIDE WONDER

Myths about tentacled sea monsters can be found in every corner of the world, from Norway to New Zealand and from the Caribbean to Japan. Could the stories be inspired by real sightings of the same strange sea creature?

WHAT COULD IT BE?

ENORMOUS SQUID?

There are, in fact, huge squid roaming the seas… only they aren't quite as enormous as the legends would have you believe. There are two species of squid that might have inspired exaggerated stories of the Kraken: the giant squid and the colossal squid.

Giant squid

Scientific name: *Architeuthis dux*

Size: Up to 39 ft. (12 m) long

Appearance: A bullet-shaped body with eight arms, two long tentacles, and a beak-like mouth

Diet: It hunts fish, crustaceans, and other squid and scavenges dead sea creatures.

Behavior: Rarely seen, as they live in the deep ocean, a live giant squid was first filmed in 2004, but they are mostly known from dead individuals washed up on shore, or body parts found in the stomachs of whales. There is still much we don't know about this creature.

Colossal squid

Scientific name: *Mesonychoteuthis hamiltoni*

Size: Up to 33 ft. (10 m) long

Appearance: A little shorter than a giant squid, but with a bigger, heavier body, it also has eight arms, two tentacles, plus the largest beak of any squid. It is the largest known invertebrate (animal without a skeleton) in the world and has the largest eyes of any animal—bigger than a basketball.

Diet: It hunts fish, crustaceans, and other squid.

Behavior: It lives in the deep Antarctic Ocean and is very rarely seen alive. Only a few colossal squid have ever been found. It can tackle larger prey than the giant squid does and is thought to be a strong, fast-moving ambush predator… but it isn't a match for a ship!

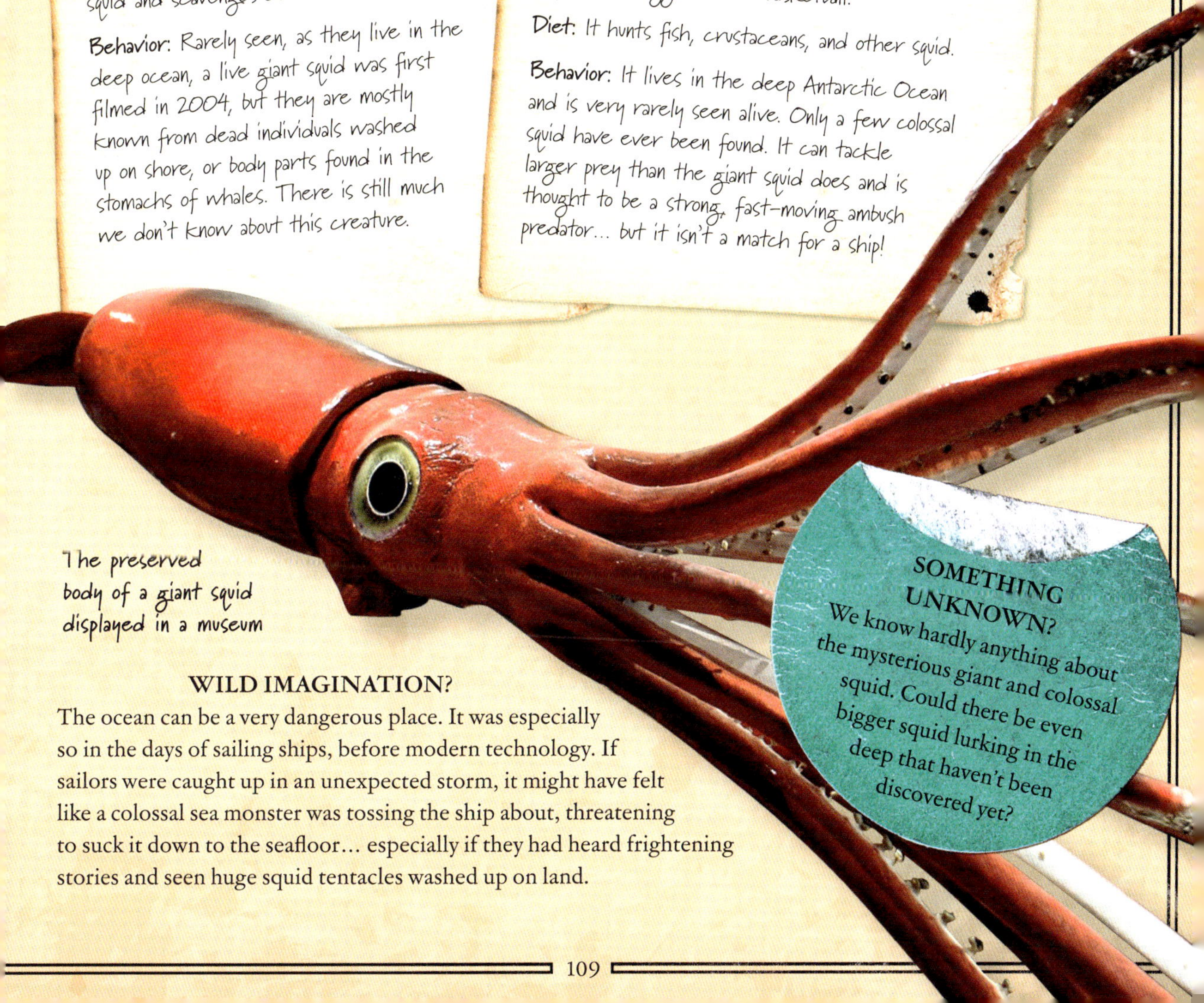

The preserved body of a giant squid displayed in a museum

SOMETHING UNKNOWN?

We know hardly anything about the mysterious giant and colossal squid. Could there be even bigger squid lurking in the deep that haven't been discovered yet?

WILD IMAGINATION?

The ocean can be a very dangerous place. It was especially so in the days of sailing ships, before modern technology. If sailors were caught up in an unexpected storm, it might have felt like a colossal sea monster was tossing the ship about, threatening to suck it down to the seafloor… especially if they had heard frightening stories and seen huge squid tentacles washed up on land.

THE GREAT BLUE HOLE

Just off the coast of the Central American country of Belize is one of the most spectacular wonders of the natural world. For many years, no one knew how long the mysterious Great Blue Hole had existed, how it was formed, or what lay at the bottom of it. But, with the help of submarines and sonar equipment, explorers have been able to dive into this strange, circular chasm to find answers.

Dwarfing a ship, the deep, dark sinkhole stands out against the surrounding shallow, turquoise water.

What is the Great Blue Hole?

What? The largest marine sinkhole in the world

Where? Lighthouse Reef atoll, Belize

How Big? More than 1,000 ft. (300 m) across

Depth? Around 410 ft. (125 m)

LAYER OF POISON

Around 300 ft. (90 m) down, explorers have discovered a layer of hydrogen sulphide, a toxic chemical that smells of rotten eggs. The water trapped below this contains no oxygen, meaning almost nothing can live there. The shells of thousands of unlucky conches that got too close to the edge litter the bottom of the sinkhole.

WHAT IS IT?

The Great Blue Hole looks so perfectly circular, it almost seems human-made, but scientists have figured out that it was created by natural processes. It's thought that it started to form around 15,000 years ago during the last ice age, when sea levels were much lower than they are today. It was originally a limestone cave on land, which flooded as the sea level rose, making the roof of the cave collapse, resulting in a feature known as a sinkhole.

SOLVED

SPIKY EVIDENCE

Scientists can be sure that the hole formed when the rock was above sea level because they have found stalactites inside it, like the one being inspected by this diver. Stalactites can only form on land from minerals left behind over hundreds and thousands of years as water drips from cave ceilings.

BIOLUMINESCENT BAYS

As you paddle a canoe through the glowing waters of a "bio bay," you would be forgiven for thinking you've entered some sort of alien landscape. But scientists now know that this ghostly, otherworldly phenomenon has a very natural cause.

Samut Sakhon Bay, Thailand

RARE PHENOMENA

There are only a handful of bioluminescent bays in the world. Some of the brightest can be found in Puerto Rico and other Caribbean islands, as well as in the US, Mexico, Southeast Asia and Australia.

As night falls, the bioluminescent water seems to come alive. In fact, the waters are gently glowing the whole time, but the effect is only seen in the dark.

Jervis Bay, New South Wales, Australia

San Diego Bay, California

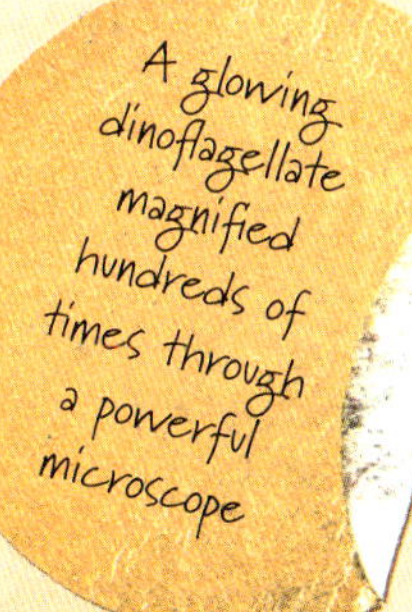

WHAT CAUSES THE GLOW?

Magical though it seems, the glow isn't caused by fairy dust, alien slime, or nuclear waste. It is all due to tiny, single-celled organisms called dinoflagellates that live in the water. They give off a special chemical that glows when it comes in contact with oxygen.

AFRICA

Africa is already home to some of Earth's biggest and fiercest animals. But with rumors of mysterious beasts resembling dinosaurs lurking in the lush jungles, cryptozoologists come here hoping to see something extra special on their safaris. Daring travelers will also need courage to explore Egypt's pyramids, where curses have supposedly befallen greedy grave robbers, or to set foot in the Castle of Good Hope, South Africa's oldest—and most haunted—building. One thing's for sure: there are still many mysteries to be uncovered in this vast continent.

KEY

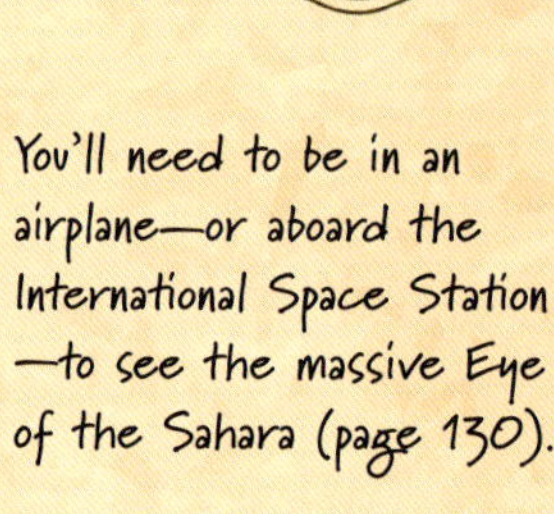

You'll need to be in an airplane—or aboard the International Space Station—to see the massive Eye of the Sahara (page 130).

1
2
3
4
7
8
9
10
11
12
The beautiful, pink Lake Natron is worth a visit just to see the incredible flocks of flamingos that live in its harsh, salty waters (page 131).

THE PYRAMIDS OF GIZA

The three giant pyramids of Giza have stood for some 4,500 years, rising out of the desert like something from another planet. They have been a source of wonder ever since they were built. Though we know the pyramids were the burial chambers of early Egyptian pharaohs, there remain many mysteries. How could ancient people have built such colossal structures, unlike anything else seen on the planet before or since? And what could be the meaning of all the secret shafts and chambers within?

How were they built?

There have been many theories about how Egypt's pyramids were built:

- The massive stone blocks may have been transported from the River Nile by raft on a canal that has since dried up.
- The blocks might have been slid to the building site on wet sand.
- Builders may have created a sloping bank of earth and pulled the blocks up using a pulley system.

The three large pyramids were built between 2600 and 2500 BCE for the pharaohs (from the left) Menkaure, Khafre, and Khufu. The three smaller pyramids were built for Egyptian queens.

SHINING BEACONS

Today, the pyramids' surface looks rough, worn down by thousands of years of desert winds. But when they were newly built, they would have been covered in polished limestone and capped with gold at the top, making them dazzle with glory in the African sun.

The pyramid shape may have represented the Sun's rays shining down, or the first mound of earth that the Egyptians believed rose up from the sea to create the world.

WHAT MYSTERIES REMAIN?

ALIEN ASSISTANCE

Some people have claimed that the ancient Egyptians had help building the pyramids... from aliens! They think that the technology used must have been so sophisticated that it could only have come from another planet.

SKILLED BUILDERS

It was once assumed that the Egyptian rulers must have used huge numbers of enslaved people to build such massive structures, but experts now think that skilled builders came together from across Egypt to help erect them, living in a temporary city nearby.

Skilled builders also created the complex's famous statue of the Sphinx in around 2550 BCE.

ALIGNED TO THE STARS?

The stars were very important to ancient Egyptians, and it's long been thought that the pyramids' positions might have a link to the night sky. Mysterious shafts in the Great Pyramid of Khufu (below) are thought to line up with Orion's Belt and where the North Star would have shone during ancient Egyptian times. Connecting the burial chamber to the night sky above was perhaps a route for the pharaoh's spirit to soar up into the stars.

HIDDEN VOIDS

The pyramids are filled with secret rooms and passageways, believed to have been put there to outsmart would-be thieves trying to steal the treasures left for the pharaohs' afterlives. Scientists have now used imaging technology to discover that the pyramids also contain hidden voids—huge, empty spaces locked deep within the monuments. The purpose of the voids remains a mystery, with experts guessing that they might have helped support the pyramids' structure, or perhaps held a special spiritual meaning.

THE CURSE OF TUTANKHAMUN

In November 1922, archaeologist Howard Carter made a momentous discovery. After years of searching, he had finally found the mysterious lost tomb of Pharaoh Tutankhamun. When he broke through the sealed doorway, it was the first time anyone had seen inside for nearly 3,000 years. Through the small opening, he glimpsed gold treasures glinting in the light. But, according to legend, there was something else lurking in the tomb: a deadly curse that would befall anyone who entered...

Who was Tutankhamun?

- An Egyptian pharaoh, now affectionately known as King Tut
- He became pharaoh aged just nine.
- He died aged about 18, in 1323 BCE.
- His tomb is cut into the hillside in an area known as the Valley of the Kings.
- Experts studying King Tut's mummy think he may have died from an illness such as malaria, injuries from a chariot crash, or a bone disease.
- Some people think he may even have been murdered.
- His death was probably sudden—his small tomb was finished quickly and was much more modest than the kind usually built for pharaohs.

Items in the tomb included a golden throne, chariots, furniture, jewelry, figurines, clothing, makeup, and baskets of food. In total, there were more than 5,000 objects.

INSIDE THE TOMB

Tutankhamun's tomb was special because it was the only tomb to be discovered that was almost untouched, and not ransacked by grave robbers. Inside, the archaeologists found a grand, multi-layered coffin holding the mummy of Tutankhamun, along with many treasures and everyday items that the ancient Egyptians thought would be needed in the afterlife.

COVERED OVER

The ancient Egyptians soon forgot their teenage pharaoh. Within a few years, they had built another tomb right on top of his, blocking the entrance with rubble. This might explain why grave robbers had overlooked his grave. It took Howard Carter years to finally track down where the king was buried. The image below shows him opening the shrine where Tutankhamum lay buried in a gold death mask.

A GRUESOME DEATH

One of the first people to enter King Tut's tomb was the very rich Lord Carnarvon, who was a keen Egyptologist and had helped pay for the expedition. Shockingly, only a few months later, on April 5, 1923, Lord Carnarvon died. He was aged just 56. It was thought that the cause was a mosquito bite that had become infected. In a time before antibiotics, this seemingly small injury led to fatal blood poisoning and pneumonia. But with his death so soon after the discovery of Tutankhamun's tomb, it sparked shock and excitement across the world. Had an ancient curse caught up with Lord Carnarvon?

Lord Carnarvon pictured relaxing in 1923, shortly before his mysterious death

Turn the page to read more about the curse...

WAS THE TOMB CURSED?

Soon after King Tut's tomb was discovered, a rumor started to spread across the world. It was said that, by entering the sacred tomb, a curse had been unleashed that would strike down the team and all connected with taking the pharaoh out of his resting place. Over the next few years, some of those involved did seem to suffer an early death. Could there have been some truth behind the spooky rumor?

MORE VICTIMS

It has been claimed that many other people fell victim to the curse because they had had some connection to the pharaoh's tomb. The alleged victims included:

- Sir Archibald Douglas Reid, who was said to have X-rayed the mummy
- Arthur Mace, who was part of the archaeological dig
- Egyptian aristocrat Ali Kamel Fahmy Bey, who had visited the tomb
- Albert Lythgoe, head Egyptologist at a museum in New York, who had viewed the open sarcophagus

However, most of these deaths happened years after the discovery of Tutankhamun's tomb, and plenty of those who entered the tomb didn't suffer an early or unusual death. But the coincidence of so many deaths was enough to convince many people that there really was a curse.

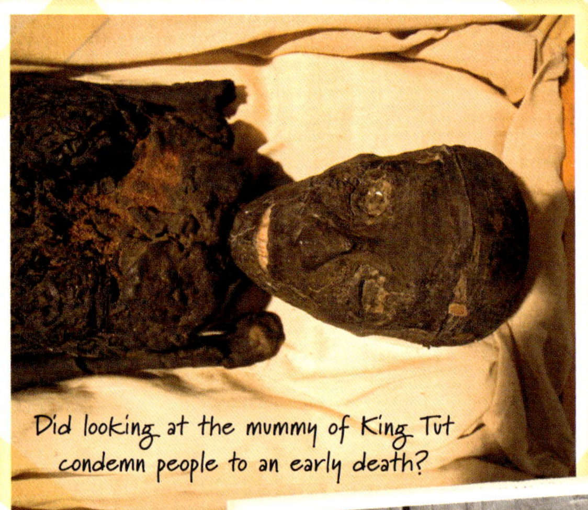

Did looking at the mummy of King Tut condemn people to an early death?

Or was it the breaking of the seal that unleashed the curse?

Howard Carter examining Tut's sarcophagus

SPREADING THE CURSE

Howard Carter is said to have given one of his friends an item from the tomb. Not long after, the friend's house burnt down. After the house was rebuilt, it was flooded! Was it the curse… or just bad luck?

A gilded statue of Tut taken from the tomb

FALSE RUMOR

Not long after the tomb was found, a rumor was started by a writer named Marie Corelli (left), who felt it was bad luck to have taken the treasures from King Tut's tomb. She claimed that a curse was engraved on the tomb wall, which translated as "death comes on wings to he who enters the tomb of a pharaoh." However, this turned out to be completely made up! There was no such inscription. If the tomb was cursed, then its Egyptian builders must have kept it a secret.

Today, Tut (right) is back in his burial chamber protected by a glass case.

EVIL SPIRIT

Sherlock Holmes novelist Arthur Conan Doyle believed King Tut's tomb was cursed by an evil spirit created by Egyptian priests to protect the mummy.

DEADLY FUNGUS

Scientists have discovered that some deadly mold spores are able to survive for an extremely long time—even thousands of years—and may have been present in the tomb. If so, it's possible they could have infected someone who breathed them in. Some have speculated that the ancient Egyptians may have even placed spores there on purpose, as a deadly—and invisible—poison to punish grave robbers. But if Lord Carnarvon really was infected by an ancient fungus, it was one that Howard Carter and the other members of the dig weren't affected by.

CURSE OR NO CURSE?

So what do you think? Was Lord Carnarvon cursed… or just unlucky? Would you risk entering an ancient Egyptian tomb? If you're worried that a curse has been cast on any would-be grave robbers, then it might be a sign that you should keep your hands to yourself!

THE DOGON AND SIRIUS

In a remote part of Mali, the Dogon people are reported to have knowledge of the stars and planets that has sparked rumors of "ancient astronauts" visiting from a distant star. The Dogon's mythology tells of an alien encounter, thousands of years ago. For some, their knowledge of astronomy proves this must be true. Others argue that there must be a more straightforward explanation...

WHO ARE THE DOGON?

The Dogon are an ancient ethnic group of more than half a million people who live in the countries of Mali and Burkina Faso. They have a rich culture and oral tradition, meaning that religious stories have been passed down by word of mouth over generations. Today, some Dogon are Muslim or Christian, but most still follow their traditional religion.

The Dogon are known for their dances performed wearing masks.

AMPHIBIOUS ALIENS

The Dogon's religious stories tell that, thousands of years ago, strange amphibious beings similar to merpeople traveled from the star Sirius to Earth in some sort of craft. The Dogon call these beings the Nommos. They were said to have green hair and skin, with red eyes and forked tongues. According to the Dogon, the Nommos taught them what they know about the stars and planets.

VISITING THE DOGON

A French scientist called Marcel Griaule visited the Dogon several times between 1931 and 1956. He listened to their religious stories and realized that the Dogon knew the star Sirius A has a twin, Sirius B. They also knew that Saturn has rings and Jupiter has moons. None of these can be seen with the naked eye. How could the Dogon know about them when they didn't have telescopes? Could their incredible legends of the Nommos really be based on fact?

The bright star Sirius A (left) has a much dimmer, smaller "twin."

HOW DID THEY KNOW?

How the Dogon came to know about Sirius B is shrouded in mystery. There are some earthly possibilities, though…

ANCIENT KNOWLEDGE?

Perhaps long ago, some of the Dogon or other peoples, such as the ancient Egyptians, had invented a simple sort of telescope or lens that had allowed them to glimpse space objects. If so, that special knowledge could have been passed down over time and become part of the Dogon's religious beliefs. But if that's true, what happened to that ancient technology? Why was that not passed down too?

The ancient Egyptians made observations of the night sky, which they recorded in their art.

It took the invention of giant, powerful telescopes for Sirius B to be discovered in 1862.

MODERN KNOWLEDGE?

Perhaps in the 19th or early 20th century, people from elsewhere could have visited the Dogon and told them about Sirius B and the planets. This knowledge could have then been mixed into the Dogon people's traditional beliefs over time.

COINCIDENCE?

Others believe that Griaule (shown on the left) and other scientists have misrepresented the views of the Dogon to match their own beliefs. They argue that the similarity between the Dogon's legends and what astronomers have discovered with telescopes is just coincidence.

ALIEN ENCOUNTERS

Some people are convinced that the Dogon's stories and star knowledge show they have been visited by aliens. If that's true, perhaps they'll return one day and share some more knowledge with us! Let's hope they're friendly…

THE MOKELE-MBEMBE

The last of the colossal sauropod dinosaurs died out 65 million years ago, so wouldn't it be incredible to find one still lurking in the remote jungles of Africa? It's a tantalising thought, and one that has inspired many explorers to search for the shy and mysterious Mokele-Mbembe, a legendary river-dwelling monster said to live in the Congo region of Central Africa.

Eyewitness descriptions

So what does the Mokele-Mbembe look like? With sightings dating back hundreds of years, here are some descriptions of the mysterious, shy cryptid:

- It has a long neck like a dinosaur.
- It has a horn or a single tooth.
- It walks on four legs.
- It lives in the rivers, lakes, and swamps of the Congo Basin.
- It is about the size of an elephant.
- It has smooth gray-brown skin.
- It has a long, strong tail like an alligator.
- It hides in the caves along the banks of rivers, keeping out of sight.
- It eats plants but will attack people if they get too close.

The vast Congo jungle has plenty of room for the monster to hide.

EVADING CAPTURE

Despite numerous sightings, it has proved impossible to find physical proof that the creature exists. In 1776, French missionaries reported finding huge, clawed tracks (left), but nothing else is known about what might have made them. In 1981, an expedition to the Congo to find proof of the Mokele-Mbembe came back empty-handed. Then, in 1992, a Japanese film crew captured 15 fuzzy seconds of what they claimed was footage of the Mokele-Mbembe. However, sceptics say that you can't see for sure what is in the video, and it could just be an elephant.

WHAT COULD IT BE?

Mokele-Mbembe means "one who stops the flow of rivers" in the local Lingala language. It would have to be a pretty enormous creature to block an entire river!

A DINOSAUR?

Some people believe the Mokele-Mbembe is a dinosaur that has somehow survived for millions of years in Africa's jungles. Scientist point out that the climate and habitats of Africa have changed many times since the dinosaurs went extinct, making the survival of a species almost impossible. They also argue that any big dinosaur-like creature roaming the waterways of the Congo would have been captured by now. After all, the big animals of Africa are all well-known to humans—or are they?

A rhino wallowing in a river

OR JUST A RHINO?

One explanation for sightings of the Mokele-Mbembe is that people glimpsed a rhino wading in the river. Rhinos aren't usually found in the Congo Basin, so they wouldn't be a familiar sight, but they do occasionally stray into the area. Though a rhino doesn't exactly match all the descriptions of this elusive cryptid, perhaps stories of the sightings have become exaggerated over time. Whatever the truth, the legend lives on and cryptozoologists continue to scour the African jungle in search of the Mokele-Mbembe.

THE NANDI BEAR

A bear-like creature is said to stalk the forests of Kenya and East Africa. Claimed to be responsible for ferocious night-time attacks on people and animals, this feared animal is known as the Nandi bear. Is it a creature that escaped scientific attention or just a myth?

WHERE'S THE BEAR?

Although eyewitnesses report the creature as looking like a bear, no species of bear has been known to live in Africa since prehistoric times. Could there really be an undiscovered bear on the loose that has evaded capture?

What does it look like?

- A large animal, as big as a lion
- A sloping back, like a hyena or bear
- Shaggy, reddish fur
- Can rear up on its hind legs
- Leaves huge paw prints with three clawed toes
- Makes a howling noise

MANY NAMES

The Nandi bear is known by several other names in local languages, including Kerit and Chemosit. Regardless of its name, no bear-like creature has ever been captured, killed, or caught on camera. So what could explain all the sightings of the so-called Nandi bear?

WHAT COULD IT BE?

MISTAKEN IDENTITY?

Some zoologists claim that many reported sightings have turned out to be a spotted hyena or a honey badger (such as the one on the right). Although they don't completely fit the description of the Nandi bear, they have lots of features in common, and it's possible that a person could misidentify a fierce creature when surprised or under attack. In fact, it's likely that witnesses are describing more than one type of animal.

HAIRY HYENA?

In 1960, an unknown long-haired animal was shot and killed. Its description sounded a lot like the fabled Nandi bear, and its skeleton, skin, and casts of its paw prints were sent to a museum in Nairobi, Kenya, to be studied. The museum curator thought that the animal was a brown hyena—a species from Southern Africa (left), which would be considered very unusual if it turned up in East Africa. Sadly, we'll never know for sure. The specimen was sent by sea to the Natural History Museum in London but it got lost on the way.

GORILLA GOSSIP?

It has been suggested that stories of the Nandi bear could have started with descriptions of a gorilla (right), but gorillas live far away in Central Africa. It's easy to imagine how descriptions could become muddled in the days before photography and video.

EXTINCT ANIMAL?

Some have suggested that the Nandi bear might have been an unknown kind of bear or another type of animal that has gone extinct since it was sighted in the 1800s. If so, this would explain why far fewer sightings have been reported in the last century. *Chalicotherium* (left) was a prehistoric plant-eater that closely matches descriptions of the Nandi bear... but it is thought to have died out in Africa around 1 million years ago.

KONGAMATO

Across Central and Southern Africa, there are whispers of a fearsome flying creature on the loose. With a name meaning "breaker of boats," local legends tell of a pterodactyl-like animal that can attack and capsize small ships, sometimes killing those on board. Its name? Kongamato.

MORE THAN A MYTH?

While many dismiss stories of the Kongamato as myth, some people think it could actually exist and have tried to track it down. In 1932, a British explorer named Frank H. Welland visited the Jiundu swamps in Zambia and listened to the locals' accounts of the Kongamato. They believed it to be a real animal. Welland claimed to have shown the locals pictures of a prehistoric pterosaur—or flying reptile—which they recognised as the Kongamato.

Is Kongamato a pterosaur, like the ones shown here?

The Kaonde tribe of Zambia reportedly used to carry charms, known as *muchi wa Kongamato*, as protection against the creature when they had to cross certain rivers.

What does it look like?

- Narrow head
- Long beak filled with small, sharp teeth
- Leathery skin instead of feathers
- Long, thin tail
- Eagle-like feet
- Wings more like a bat's than a bird's
- 3–7 ft. (1–2 m) wingspan
- 4.5 ft. (1.4 m) long body
- Reddish-black color

WHAT COULD IT BE?

A PTEROSAUR?

Descriptions of the Kongamato do sound a lot like a prehistoric flying reptile, or pterosaur, that was around at the time of the dinosaurs. But all scientific evidence shows that they died out when Earth was hit by an asteroid 65 million years ago. If the Kongamato really is a living pterosaur, how could the species have survived for so long? Why haven't any of the creatures been found, alive or dead?

A BIG BIRD?

Sceptics think there is no such thing as the Kongamato. Instead, some think that a tall bird called a saddle-billed stork (left) may have been mistaken for the monster. Although the stork doesn't have all the features of a Kongamato, the descriptions could have grown more fanciful as the legend has been retold over the centuries.

AHOOL!

The Kongamato is similar to another cryptid from the island of Java in Southeast Asia. The Ahool is named after its distinctive cry—"A-HOOOoool!"—and is said to have a head like a monkey, gray fur, big claws, and huge, leathery wings reaching 10 ft. (3 m) across. Visually, the descriptions are very similar to the (slightly smaller) large flying fox (right), a giant bat with a 5 ft (1.5 m) wingspan. Its call is very much like that of the rare Javan wood owl. Perhaps someone saw a bat and heard an owl at the same time and mixed them together to create the new creature.

HAUNTED AFRICA

The jungles, savannah, and deserts of Africa are well known for their deadly dangers: scorching heat, fierce wild animals, and biting insects. But it's not just the natural world that poses a risk. From North Africa to the continent's southern tip, there are creepy tales of ghosts and ghouls.

WHITE DESERT, EGYPT

Though deserts are notoriously risky places to travel, the strange White Desert may be more dangerous than most—it is said to be haunted by the ghost of Pharaoh Akhenaten (reigned c.1353–36 BCE), the father of Tutankhamun—who has his own spooky legacy (page 116). Akhenaten's spirit was cursed by priests to wander the desert forever because he had tried to get rid of the traditional Egyptian gods. Some say that the pharaoh's anguished wails can be heard on the desert winds.

The White Desert gets its name from its bizarre looking chalky white rocks.

ERASMUS CASTLE, SOUTH AFRICA

Nicknamed the Haunted House, or Die Spookhuis in the Afrikaans language, Erasmus Castle (right) is a grand house built on a hill in South Africa in the 1890s. Visitors claim to have seen the ghost of a young girl, a man sitting in an armchair, and a lady wearing a Victorian nightgown. People also claim to have heard unexplained footsteps and noticed lights turning off on their own.

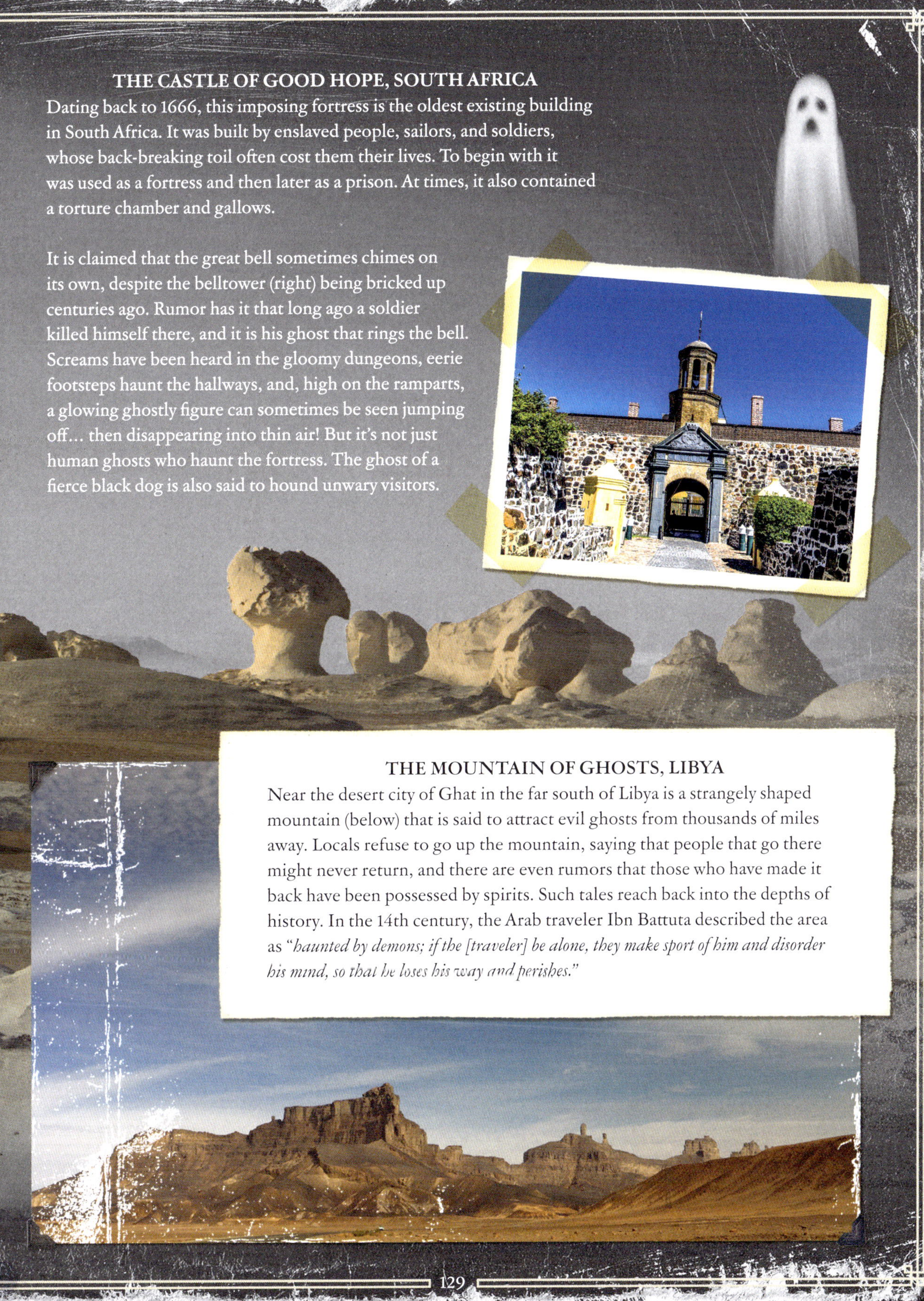

THE CASTLE OF GOOD HOPE, SOUTH AFRICA

Dating back to 1666, this imposing fortress is the oldest existing building in South Africa. It was built by enslaved people, sailors, and soldiers, whose back-breaking toil often cost them their lives. To begin with it was used as a fortress and then later as a prison. At times, it also contained a torture chamber and gallows.

It is claimed that the great bell sometimes chimes on its own, despite the belltower (right) being bricked up centuries ago. Rumor has it that long ago a soldier killed himself there, and it is his ghost that rings the bell. Screams have been heard in the gloomy dungeons, eerie footsteps haunt the hallways, and, high on the ramparts, a glowing ghostly figure can sometimes be seen jumping off… then disappearing into thin air! But it's not just human ghosts who haunt the fortress. The ghost of a fierce black dog is also said to hound unwary visitors.

THE MOUNTAIN OF GHOSTS, LIBYA

Near the desert city of Ghat in the far south of Libya is a strangely shaped mountain (below) that is said to attract evil ghosts from thousands of miles away. Locals refuse to go up the mountain, saying that people that go there might never return, and there are even rumors that those who have made it back have been possessed by spirits. Such tales reach back into the depths of history. In the 14th century, the Arab traveler Ibn Battuta described the area as "*haunted by demons; if the [traveler] be alone, they make sport of him and disorder his mind, so that he loses his way and perishes.*"

THE EYE OF THE SAHARA

As astronauts on the International Space Station gaze across the vast expanse of the Sahara Desert, they look out in particular for one breathtaking landmark: the Eye of the Sahara in Mauritania, Northwest Africa. Also known as the Richat Structure, its swirling, colorful circles look like an enormous bull's eye in the sand.

TOO BIG!

This mysterious structure is 25 miles (40 km) across. It was first discovered in the 1930s, but it is so big that it was difficult to see clearly from ground level. No one was certain what it was. However, its unique shape and pattern became clear when viewed from space.

A UFO LANDING PAD?

At first, scientists thought the Eye was a meteor's impact crater, but further study has shown that's not the case. In fact, the beautiful landmark has sparked a few wild rumors. Some have suggested that the Eye could be a landing pad for alien spacecraft. Others have claimed it is the site of the lost city of Atlantis (page 98), because the Greek philosopher Plato described Atlantis as having rings of water and land.

There's no evidence that UFOs are taking off and landing on the Eye.

SOLVED

WHAT IS IT REALLY?

In fact, the strange structure is a dome of layers in Earth's crust that has worn away over millions of years, revealing rings of different sedimentary and igneous rocks. Geologists think that the dome began to form more than 100 million years ago, as Africa and South America began to pull apart from each other.

A LAKE OF STONE

Lake Natron in Tanzania has a strange and eerie power: it can seemingly turn animals to stone. But this isn't witchcraft—it has been discovered that the lake naturally contains a large amount of a mineral that turns the waters into a deadly potion.

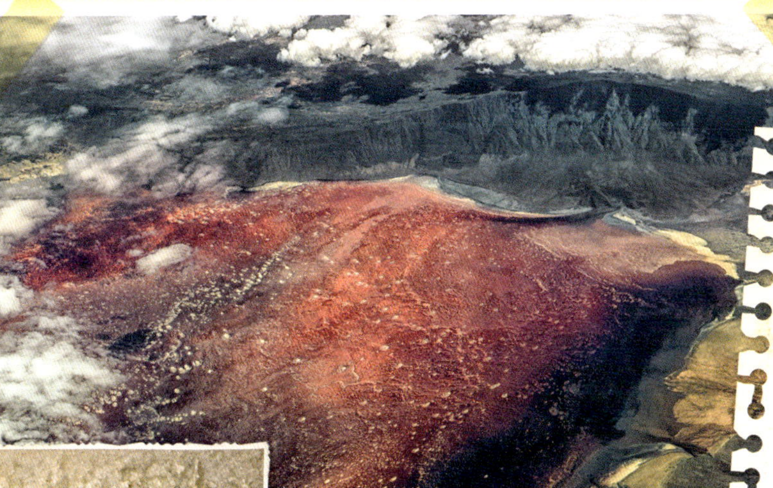

The lake is colored pink by the salt-eating microorganisms that live in it.

SOLVED

DEATH TRAP

Water flows into Lake Natron but can't flow out. Over time, as the water evaporates, the salts and other minerals left behind build up. The lake contains a lot of a mineral called natron, which is extremely alkaline. The toxic waters mean near instant death to any bird or mammal that falls into the lake. Unfortunately, creatures flying close by are often confused by the lake's pink, glassy surface, which they find difficult to spot.

STATUES ON THE SHORE

Something very strange happens to bodies of the lake's unlucky victims. Rather than rot away or be eaten, as a dead creature in a normal lake might be, the bodies of animals in Lake Natron are coated with the lake's alkaline salts, making them look like they've turned to stone. Eventually, they wash up on shore, hardened like statues.

Natron was the substance used by ancient Egyptians to preserve their mummies.

LUCKY FOR SOME

Although Lake Natron is deadly for some, its beautiful, pink waters are a haven for vast groups of flamingos (right), which raise their chicks here every year. Few animals are able to tolerate such harsh conditions, but these remarkable birds can. Far from any predators, they eat the pink microorganisms that grow in the water—which cause the bird's feathers to turn pink.

If you visit Thailand in the fall, make sure to stop by the Mekong River and try to catch a glimpse of the famous Naga fireballs for yourself (page 152).

KEY

N
W
E
S

ASIA

As the world's largest continent, Asia has accumulated a huge number of mysteries over the centuries. These range from Kazakhstan's ancient geoglyphs, thought to be 10,000 years old, to Turkmenistan's burning "Door to Hell" that opened up around 50 years ago. Adventurers will also have plenty of curious cryptids to look out for, from the death worm fabled to hide in the scorching Gobi Desert, to the legendary Yeti that roams the Himalayan mountains. So get ready for sun and snow, towns and tundra—and mysteries everywhere!

THE TUNGUSKA EVENT

On June 30, 1908, something bright and shining plummeted to Earth and a huge explosion rocked the Siberian forest, flattening millions of trees and making the earth shake far across Russia. To this day, nobody understands exactly what had happened.

EYEWITNESS ACCOUNTS

- At around 7:17 a.m., a very bright, bluish light is seen speeding across the sky, leaving a trail behind it. As it reaches the horizon, a bright flash of light is followed by plumes of black smoke and fire.
- About 10 minutes later a huge explosion is heard. Witnesses feel a massive shockwave, powerful enough to break windows and push people over, even hundreds of miles away.
- Further explosions are heard, described as being like cannons or thunder.
- When people later inspected the area, they found that trees had been flattened and burned for miles around, as shown in these photos.
- For several days, bright clouds were seen in the night sky over Asia and Europe.

STUDYING THE BLAST SITE

It was another 10 years before scientists visited the Tunguska area to investigate what may have caused the extraordinary explosion. Assuming it was an asteroid, they expected to find an impact crater—but there was none!

LUCKY ESCAPE

In total, the explosion destroyed more than 800 sq miles (2,000 sq km) of forest, flattening around 80 million trees. Thankfully, only two or three people died. It's very lucky that the event happened in such a remote area. If such a massive explosion happened over a large city, it could have killed millions of people.

WHAT CAUSED THE TUNGUSKA EVENT?

As this object enters Earth's atmosphere, it leaves a long flaming trail as it burns up.

GLANCING BLOW?

Some scientists think a large asteroid may have hurtled toward Earth at a very shallow angle, but glanced off Earth's atmosphere and went back off into space—which is why it didn't leave behind an impact crater.

COMET?

Other scientists argue that it could have been a different type of visitor from outer space: a small comet (above), made of dust, ice, and frozen gases, which vaporised on impact with Earth's atmosphere, leaving no crater. This theory helps explain the bright skies seen for days after the event but doesn't explain how the mystery space object seemed to have remained in one piece until reaching the lower part of the atmosphere.

METEOR AIR BLAST?

A stony asteroid would enter Earth's atmosphere at a colossal speed. Usually, it would plummet to the ground in one piece, leaving an impact crater. But it could be possible that the huge pressure and high temperatures that built up as the asteroid sped through the sky caused it to explode in midair, creating a huge shockwave. Instead of raining down, the minuscule pieces of meteor flew up into the atmosphere, causing the strange glow seen in the skies after the event.

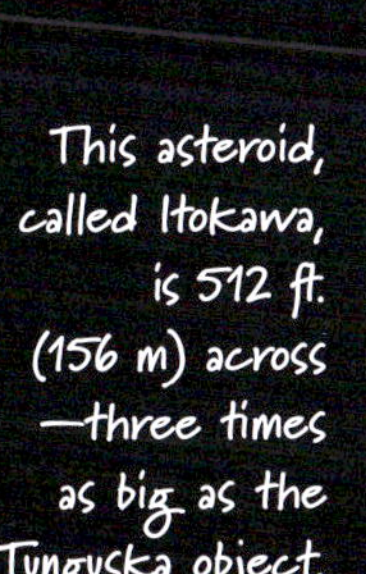

This asteroid, called Itokawa, is 512 ft. (156 m) across—three times as big as the Tunguska object.

RARE EVENT

Today, after years of research and experiments, scientists think the Tunguska Event was most likely caused by an asteroid, not a comet. Thankfully, strikes of this size are very rare. Another one is unlikely to happen for thousands of years.

STEPPE GEOGLYPHS

Nicknamed the Nazca Lines of Kazakhstan, these giant geoglyphs, or rock pictures, are a truly puzzling discovery. They range in size from 295 ft. (90 m) to a massive 1,300 ft. (400 m) long, making them difficult to see unless viewed from the air. In fact, they were only discovered in 2007, when Dmitriy Dey, an economist from Kazakhstan, was looking at Google Earth. What else do you think might be waiting to be discovered somewhere on the planet?

WHAT ARE THEY?

The geoglyphs are a collection of around 260 giant pictures laid out on the ground. They're located in the steppe, or grasslands, of northern Kazakhstan in a low-lying area known as the Turgay Basin. The designs are in a range of geometric shapes, including circles, squares, and crosses.

Archaeologists studying the earthworks think they were created during the Iron Age, around 2,800 years ago, but others guess that some of the markings might be as much as 8,000 years old.

HOW WERE THEY MADE?

Rather than being carved into the ground, like the Nazca Lines were (page 48), these massive geoglyphs were made by piling earth, rocks, and wood up on the ground. Each mound is around 3 ft. (1 m) high and 30 ft. (9 m) wide. Close-up, they look a bit like the mounds in this image on the left from a giant work of art created in the Egyptian desert in the 1990s.

WHAT WERE THEY USED FOR?

BORDERS?

The identity of who made the geoglyphs—and why—is still shrouded in mystery. Some people studying the symbols think that they may have been made by an ancient nomadic people known as the Mahandzhar. The designs may have acted as a kind of border, marking the edge of a particular people's territory.

Horse herding still takes place in Kazakhstan's grasslands.

SACRED PLACES?

The geoglyphs may have had a religious purpose, acting as a sacred place or sanctuary. Their precise shapes and layouts would suggest they had some sort of meaning for the people who made them, although no one as yet has any idea what this might be.

CALENDARS?

Traditional Kazakh life was nomadic, with people following herds of horses across the region's great expanses of steppe. The shapes may have been used as a sort of calendar, helping people to track the movements of the Sun and seasons, and so predict the movement of the animal herds.

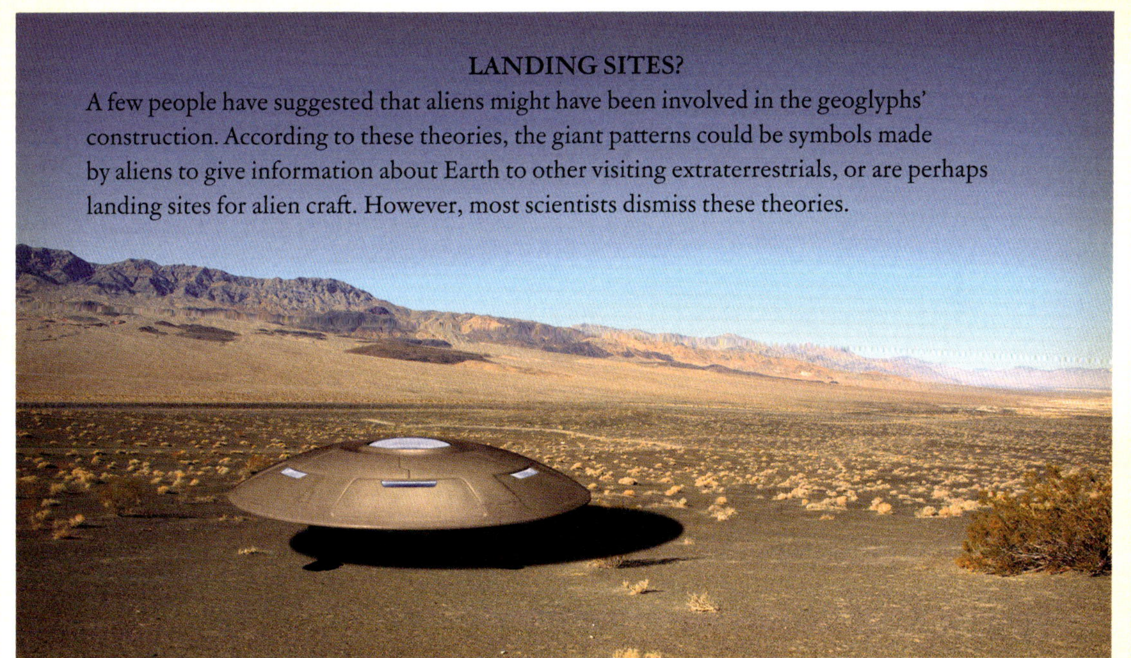

LANDING SITES?

A few people have suggested that aliens might have been involved in the geoglyphs' construction. According to these theories, the giant patterns could be symbols made by aliens to give information about Earth to other visiting extraterrestrials, or are perhaps landing sites for alien craft. However, most scientists dismiss these theories.

THE HANGING GARDENS OF BABYLON

The Seven Wonders of the Ancient World are famous structures built by the peoples of the Mediterranean world between roughly 2500 and 250 BCE. We know for sure that six of these did exist, but the seventh wonder is shrouded in mystery. Was there ever really such a place as the Hanging Gardens of Babylon?

Lush gardens with trees and flowers grow among the towers and buildings of Babylon in this recreation.

WHAT WERE THEY?

Ancient writings claim that the Hanging Gardens were built around 600 BCE, in or near the royal palace in the city of Babylon (in present-day Iraq). They were thought to be watered by a special sort of screw that pumped water out of the Euphrates River. They weren't actually "hanging." Instead, the gardens were described as built in tiers, or terraces, filled with all sorts of trees and plants.

A PIECE OF PARADISE

Though little is known about the original Hanging Gardens, over thousands of years they have become a mythical paradise filled with exotic flowers and fruit trees. Artists have imagined them overflowing with lush green plants and beautiful waterfalls. According to legend, King Nebuchadnezzar I (c. 642–562 BCE) built the hanging gardens to comfort his wife, Amytis, because she missed the green mountains of her homeland.

King Nebuchadnezzar II shown looking over the city of Babylon from his palace

WHAT HAPPENED TO THE GARDENS?

VANISHED?

Even though most of the Seven Wonders have been destroyed, archaeologists have still found plenty of evidence that they did exist. But the Hanging Gardens of Babylon seem to have mysteriously disappeared without a trace. Despite years combing the ruins of ancient Babylon (right), no one has found anything that points to exactly where the gardens might have been.

JUST A MYTH?

Although later Greek and Roman writers described the legendary gardens, they were not mentioned in any Babylonian writings from the time. Some people think that the Hanging Gardens were just a wonderful story, passed down over centuries.

LOCATION MIX-UP?

Another theory is that the Hanging Gardens really did exist, but not in Babylon. They may have been built 280 miles (450 km) away in Nineveh (below), the capital of the Assyrian Empire, now also in Iraq. Evidence suggests the ancient city used a system of aqueducts to carry water from the mountains to the royal palace, which could have been used to water lush gardens. Nineveh was later called the "New Babylon," which might help to explain the mix-up.

GREEN-FINGERED KING

Sennacherib, king of Nineveh (c. 745–681 BCE), was known to have a grand palace garden. He called it "a wonder for all peoples" and described how screws were used to draw up water for the plants. Perhaps the legendary gardens should be renamed the Hanging Gardens of Nineveh!

Known as an Archimedes' screw, this ancient device was used to raise water from rivers.

THE MONGOLIAN DEATH WORM

Imagine you're exploring the cold, dry Gobi Desert in Mongolia. You hear stories of a sausage-shaped creature, more than two feet long, which "has no head nor leg" and "is so poisonous that merely to touch it means instant death." Though there is no concrete evidence such an animal exists, would you take your chances, or would you watch very carefully where you put your feet?

TUNNELING TERROR

This grotesque-sounding creature is the Mongolian death worm, known as *olgoi-khorkhoi* in the Mongolian language. According to local legend, the cryptid can kill by spraying venom or by producing an electric shock. It travels underground, creating waves of sand on the desert surface, and rarely emerges. Maybe this explains why there are so few sightings, and why many people don't believe it exists at all.

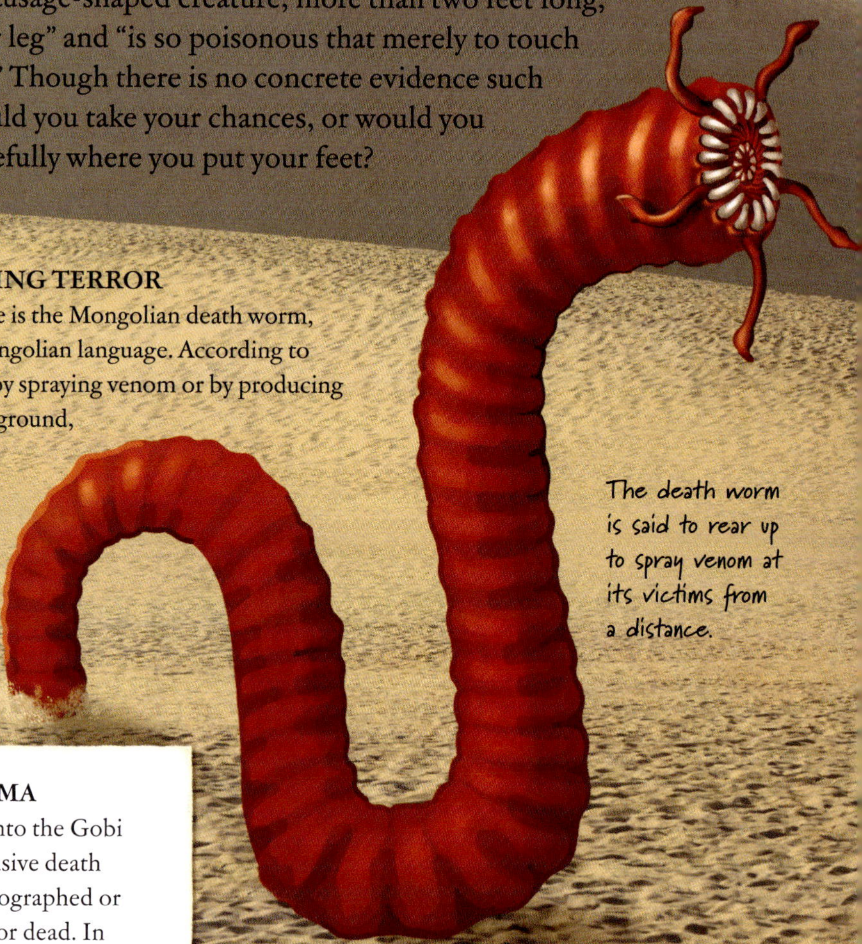

The death worm is said to rear up to spray venom at its victims from a distance.

ELUSIVE ENIGMA

Despite many expeditions into the Gobi Desert to hunt down the elusive death worm, no one has ever photographed or captured the creature, alive or dead. In fact, many stories of the creature seem to come from people who have heard about it from others, rather than seeing it with their own eyes.

WHAT COULD IT BE?

A LEGLESS LIZARD?

Although it's exciting to think that such a deadly creature could lurk under the desert sands, perhaps a more likely explanation is that the story is based on sightings of other real desert species, such as legless lizards. The burrowing skink (right) is a worm-like lizard that leaves trails in the desert sand, just like the death worm is said to. The only trouble is—the lizard is just 4 in. (11 cm) long, and lives in the Namib Desert in Africa, not the Gobi. Could there be a larger version yet to be discovered in Asia?

BURROWING SNAKE?

Some believe that tales of the death worm may be based on a type of burrowing snake called a desert sand boa (left), which does live in the Gobi. However, it isn't venomous, but instead kills prey by constricting it. So its description doesn't quite match the lethal reputation of the much-feared Mongolian death worm.

BIG INFLUENCE

Even if the death worm has yet to be confirmed by science—or perhaps doesn't exist—it's still had a major influence on popular culture. Numerous fictional creatures are said to be based on it, including the sandworms from the science fantasy novel *Dune* (1965), the desert-dwelling graboids from the horror film *Tremors* (1990), and the purple worm character from the Dungeons and Dragons game. In 2010, a TV movie called *Mongolian Death Worm* was released.

A depiction of a sandworm in the novel Dune

THE BURNING DOOR TO HELL

In the middle of the Karakum Desert in Turkmenistan is a sight that is both beautiful and terrifying: a massive burning hole in the ground that never goes out. This is the Darvaza Gas Crater. It has been alight for decades, but no one is sure when or how it started.

WHAT IS IT?

The Darvaza Gas Crater is a giant sinkhole that has been leaking burning methane gas for years. It is about 200–230 ft. (60–70 m) across and about 100 ft. (30 m) deep. Despite several attempts to put out the burning gas crater, none has been successful. In 2022, Turkmenistan's president ordered experts to figure out a way to extinguish the flames, but no one has come up with a solution yet.

This is an artist's impression of the time, in 2019, when the president of Turkmenistan appeared on TV doing donuts in a car around the crater to prove that, despite rumors, he wasn't dead!

MYSTERIOUS BEGINNINGS

It isn't clear when the crater appeared or how it came to be burning. You might think that something like this would have made the news as soon as the fire started. In fact, there are no written records available that mention what happened. Any evidence was probably kept top-secret by the Soviet Union, which controlled Turkmenistan at the time. Some say the crater appeared in 1971 and was lit soon after by Soviet geologists. But geologists in Turkmenistan say that the crater opened in the late 1960s but wasn't lit until the 1980s.

HOW DID IT START?

ACCIDENTALLY?

The burning question is, how did this massive fire start in the first place? Most people think the crater opened up accidentally when the site was being drilled for gas and was then set alight by Soviet authorities to stop it from exploding. However, the authorities probably thought the gases would burn off within a few weeks. Instead, it is still burning many decades later, and shows no sign of going out.

HIT BY LIGHTNING?

Some think that the crater wasn't set alight by people at all, but was actually sparked by a lightning strike.

"Standing at the bottom of that crater in my protective heat suit ... it's probably the closest experience that a human being can have to stepping on another world, but yet here on Earth."

—George Kourounis, Greek-Canadian Explorer

WHY BURN THE GAS?

The open crater was leaking lots of methane gas into the air. It's thought that the crater was lit on purpose to burn off the gas. If methane was left to build up in the air around the crater, then every so often it would have created a huge explosion. That sounds pretty dangerous!

HAUNTED ASIA

As the world's most populated continent, it should be no surprise that Asia is home to a great many haunted buildings and ghost stories.

ALL CHANGE PLEASE

It's rumored that in 1967, a male member of staff saw a ghost at the rural Begunkodar railway station in Northeast India. The specter was a woman wearing a white sari who danced on the platform. This story might not seem especially frightening, except for one detail: shortly afterward, the man died. This sparked fear among the other railway workers, and the supposedly haunted station was abandoned. It didn't reopen for 42 years. Though trains now run through Begunkodar once more, some passengers are still wary of ghosts and avoid using the station after sunset.

FORBIDDEN FORT

Built more than 450 years ago, the now ruined Bhangarh Fort (above left), in Northwest India, is said to be one of the country's most haunted places. Legend tells that the place was cursed by a holy man and, today, visitors often report feeling like someone—or something—is following them. It's forbidden to go into the fort after dark, with locals warning that no one who enters at night will come back out again.

ABANDONED TO ITS FATE

A grand mansion known as Chaonei No. 81 (right) stands abandoned in central Beijing. According to the stories, the political official who lived at the house fled when the Communist Party took power in China in 1949, leaving his wife behind. The wife's ghost is now said to haunt the place, devastated at being abandoned. It's also been reported that workers who came to repair the house vanished without a trace. Whether any of this is true or just tall tales, the crumbling mansion has remained deserted for decades in the middle of China's bustling capital city.

FADED LUXURY

Bokor Hill Station in Cambodia (left) was built as a luxury resort in the 1920s during French colonial times. Though it was once a place of merriment, filled with shops, bars, a hotel, and casino, this resort had a dark side: nearly 1,000 laborers are thought to have died during its construction. Decades later, it was the scene of bloody fighting during the defeat of the Khmer Rouge, the brutal communist regime that ruled the country from 1975–1979. Today, the eerie abandoned buildings are said to echo with ghostly screams.

SHIFTING SANDS

Though the ruins of Khara Khoto in China are beautiful, they are reported to be haunted by otherworldly sounds and mysterious fires. This ancient fortress was abandoned after a gruesome battle between Mongolian and Chinese forces in 1372, and the ghosts of the dead are said to have lingered there ever since. Sitting in the Gobi Desert, its ruins are steadily being buried by the drifting sand.

THE SKY CAVES

Hidden deep in the Himalayan mountain range is one of the great wonders of the world: the mysterious Sky Caves. Altogether, there are at least 10,000 human-made caves dug into the steep sides of the Mustang Valley in Nepal. Some are stacked one on top of the other, eight or nine stories high. Though we know they are thousands of years old, no one has been able to figure out the mystery of who built these incredible rooms in the rock, and how.

CAVE BODIES

In some of the stacked caves, archaeologists have discovered dozens of bodies lying on wooden beds, adorned with glass beads and copper jewelry. The cool, dry conditions partially mummified the ancient bodies, preserving many details. They are thought to be between 2,000 and 3,000 years old. In other caves, skeletons have been found from around 1,300 to 1,800 years ago. It's likely that these bodies were left in the caves as sky burials, a traditional type of burial in the region.

Some of the Mustang Caves, such as this one, have been turned into Buddhist shrines or monasteries.

This image below shows the cave entrances carved into the cliff face.

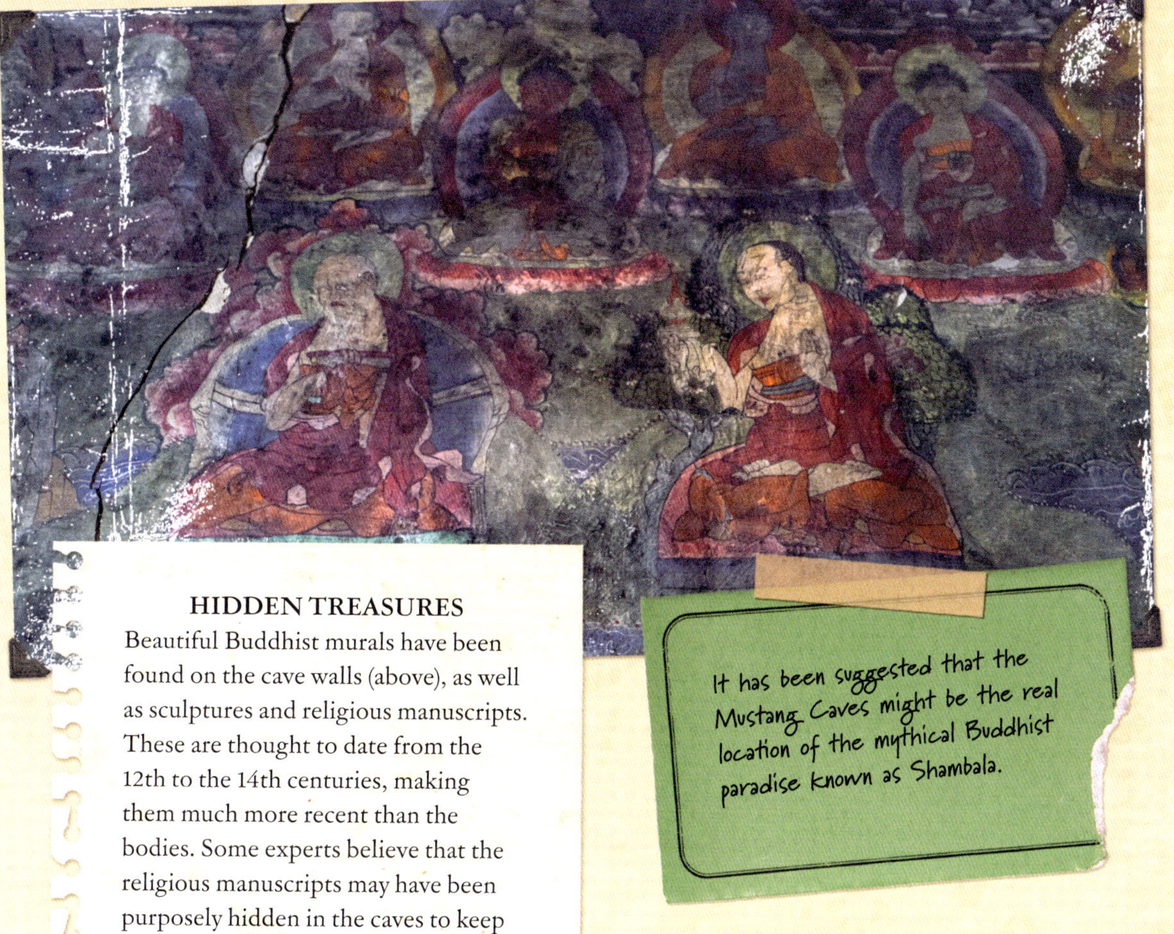

HIDDEN TREASURES

Beautiful Buddhist murals have been found on the cave walls (above), as well as sculptures and religious manuscripts. These are thought to date from the 12th to the 14th centuries, making them much more recent than the bodies. Some experts believe that the religious manuscripts may have been purposely hidden in the caves to keep them secret in times when Buddhists felt threatened. The cool, dry caves kept the forgotten documents and art safe for hundreds of years.

It has been suggested that the Mustang Caves might be the real location of the mythical Buddhist paradise known as Shambala.

WHAT WERE THE CAVES USED FOR?

- Archaeologists think that in early times, up to 3,000 years ago, the caves were used as burial chambers.
- Around 1,000 years ago, the caves began to be used as living spaces, where local people sought safety in times of war.
- By 600 years ago, the caves were used as lookout posts and places for Buddhists to meditate, but were no longer lived in.

HOW DID PEOPLE REACH THE CAVES?

Who built these caves isn't the only mystery that the Mustang Valley is keeping to itself. To this day, no one has figured out how the ancient people climbed up and down the huge, steep cliffs in order to reach the caves, let alone dig them out of the rock face. Whether they used ropes, long wooden ladders, or carved steps into the rock, no trace remains.

MORE TO DISCOVER

Archaeologists are still trying to piece together the puzzle of who built the Sky Caves. With 10,000 caves to search through, there is every chance that one day, this mystery could be solved.

THE YETI

Wind, snow, and freezing temperatures make the Himalayas a dangerous place. But the wild weather isn't the only thing you need to look out for on a trip to the world's tallest mountain range. A huge, hairy creature known as the Yeti is said to roam this region. Is it some sort of man, an ape, or a myth? No one can say for sure, but there are plenty of cryptozoologists trying to find answers to what is one of the world's best-known cryptids.

What does the Yeti look like?

- Covered in long, thick hair
- Often described as white or gray in color
- Sometimes described as black or reddish brown
- Thought to have large, very wide feet
- Stands around 6 ft. (1.8 m) or taller
- Walks upright, like a human

MODERN EVIDENCE

Legends of the Yeti have been around for thousands of years in the folklore of the Himalayan peoples. In fact, the Yeti was mainly thought of as a legendary beast until a British mountaineer called Eric Shipman photographed what he claimed to be a large, unidentified footprint in 1951. Since then, interest in the mysterious mountain ape-man has exploded, with thousands of adventurers visiting Nepal to try to catch a glimpse of the Yeti.

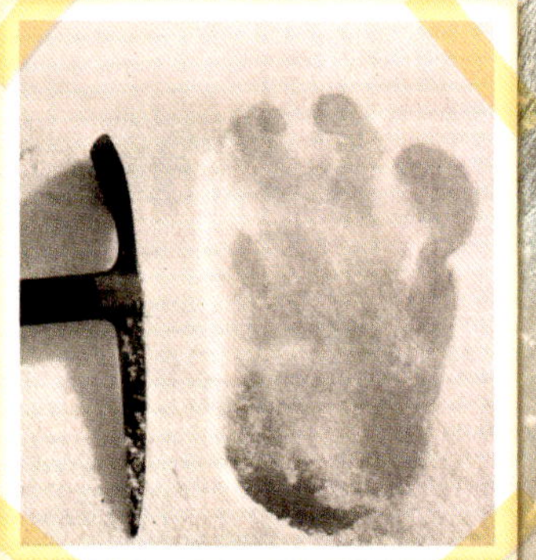

Shipman placed an ice axe next to the giant footprint to give a sense of scale. It was estimated to be around 13 in. (33 cm) long.

WHAT COULD IT BE?

MISTAKES AND HOAXES?

Some people think that reports of Yeti sightings are made up. They say that footprints are easy to fake, and that prints from known animals can change shape as the snow melts, making them seem like they are from a mysterious creature.

Depending on who you believe, this object on display in Khumjung Monastery in Nepal is either a yeti scalp or a yak hump.

EXTINCT GIANT APE?

A few people have suggested that the Yeti could be a giant ape that went extinct in prehistoric times everywhere except the Himalayan mountains. *Gigantopithecus* was a huge prehistoric ape that we know of from fossils. Although it matches the Yeti's description in some ways, it is thought to have walked on all fours. Given its colossal size, it would have struggled to walk upright.

BEARS?

There's a good chance that tracks, traces, and sightings of yetis might actually be of bears. Scientists have studied the DNA from nine samples thought to have possibly come from Yeti remains and found that one was from a dog, while the other eight were from bears. Of course, coming face-to-face with a bear in the Himalayas sounds about as terrifying as meeting a Yeti! The biggest bear in these parts, the Himalayan brown bear (below) has light-colored fur that blends easily with the snow.

The Yeti is one of the world's most famous cryptids. Though we may not have captured one, it has captured the imagination of people all over the world. While some think it is no more than an ancient myth, others think there could be a grain of truth to this snowy mystery.

THE YETI'S COUSINS

The Yeti isn't the only ape-like cryptid to have left its mighty footprints in Asia. Whispers and rumors of other humanoid creatures are told in many regions, but none has yet been scientifically proven…

NITTAEWO

Sri Lankan folklore tells of groups of small yeti-like creatures that live in caves and trees, weaving themselves nests of leaves, much like chimpanzees and gorillas do. They are said to have sharp claws, reddish fur, and walk upright, reaching a height of around 3.5 ft. (1 m). Whereas apes and monkeys have long arms for swinging through trees, the arms of the Nittaewo are described as short, more like a human's. According to some stories, the Nittaewo were wiped out around 250 years ago.

ORANG-PENDEK

This mysterious ape is said to live in the mountain jungles of Sumatra, an island in Indonesia. The beast has long arms, walks upright, and is covered in fur. Sometimes the fur is described as dark; other times it is said to be light brown or reddish. At around 3 ft (1 m) tall, it's much smaller than the Yeti and Bigfoot. The Orang-Pendek seems to share many features with the orangutan, a primate that is native to Sumatra. Is it possible that the two are related, or could it be a case of mistaken identity? Scientists have been sent on expeditions to try to photograph this mysterious cryptid.

BUKIT TIMAH MONKEY MAN

According to local folklore, this ape-like being from the forests of Singapore is immortal. First reported in 1805, it has been rarely seen since then. If it does exist, it must be an incredibly shy creature that hides away from humans. With a monkey-like face and covered in gray fur, it is said to be the height of a human and to stand and walk upright. Some have claimed that the cryptid could just be a monkey known as a crab-eating macaque (left), which has long lived near humans and occasionally walks on its hind legs when searching for food.

AMOMONGO

The people of the Philippines tell stories of a large, fierce ape that is thought to live in caves near a volcano. It is said to have long, sharp nails and be covered in white hair. Standing upright, it is about the same size as an adult human, and it has been blamed for attacks on people and farm animals.

HIBAGON

While some ape-like cryptids are known from ancient folklore, others have been sighted only in recent times. The Hibagon was first spotted on a mountain in Japan in 1970, sparking other locals to report seeing the strange creature too. It was described as walking upright, with a gorilla-shaped body and about 5 ft. (1.6 m) tall. While some think these sightings are proof that Japan has its own Bigfoot, other people have suggested it might have been a gorilla that had escaped from a zoo.

CHUCHUNYA

A dark-haired Yeti-like creature known as Chuchunya is claimed to inhabit the wilds of Siberia in Russia. Could it be a northern variety of Yeti?

BARMANOU

Allegedly spotted by shepherds in the mountains of Pakistan, this wild and hairy cryptid seems to be a cross between an ape and a human. It is said to wear animal skins, and likes to snatch unsuspecting people who get too close. According to some accounts, the creature also smells like rotting garbage. If you're lucky, you might smell him before it can catch you!

NAGA FIREBALLS

Every autumn, on a stretch of the Mekong River in Thailand, a miraculous light display amazes crowds of onlookers. Glowing pink and red orbs rise from the river and hang high in the air for a few minutes before disappearing. These are the Naga fireballs, but what causes them… ?

VIDEO EVIDENCE

There are plenty of photos and videos proving that glowing orbs do indeed rise over the Mekong River each autumn. However, people argue over whether they are a human-made hoax or an—as yet—unexplained natural phenomenon.

An artist's impression of fireballs shooting up over the river

HOLIDAY LIGHTS

Also known as Mekong lights or ghost lights, this strange phenomenon is said to be hundreds of years old. They are seen each year in October during the full Moon, at the time when Buddhists celebrate the end of a three-month period of reflection and fasting known as Vassa. Some locals have witnessed the phenomenon since childhood and say there aren't as many fireballs as there used to be.

Glowing pink balls aren't the only lights in the sky during the celebrations. Fireworks displays are also staged.

WHAT COULD IT BE?

WATER SERPENTS?

According to local beliefs, the villages on the banks of the Mekong River were created by mythical water serpents called Nagas. One legend says that the fireballs are the hot breath of the river serpents. Another tells that the Nagas shoot fireballs into the sky to rejoice at the Buddha's return from Heaven.

NATURAL GAS?

Some witnesses have suggested that the fireballs are caused by bubbles of natural gas that are released from the riverbed and catch fire when they reach the air. But others claim that it's unlikely the gas would ignite on its own and that, if it did, the fireballs wouldn't stay lit as they flew upward into the sky.

FAKES OR MISTAKES?

Some people think Naga fireballs aren't a natural phenomenon at all. They say flare guns are being fired from the other side of the river, in Laos. Others argue that images of the flares don't look like the fireballs they have seen. They point out that the fireballs come out of different places in the river, not just one side. One of the problems with identifying the phenomenon is that the sky is full of lights at this time. Many people release lanterns into the air to mark the end of Vassa, like the ones in the image below. Could these be mistaken for fireballs?

ENJOY THE SHOW

For many locals, the fireballs are a sacred phenomenon and a sign that the Nagas still bless this stretch of the Mekong River. Until someone proves the lights are caused by people or nature, perhaps it's best to look up into the night sky and enjoy the breathtaking wonder.

YAMASHITA'S LOST TREASURE

When the Japanese army occupied the Philippines during World War II, it was accused of looting a huge amount of gold and other valuables, hiding them away in secret locations across the country. According to legend, soldiers buried a vast fortune of riches in underground caves and tunnels. They planned to go back for it after the war, but never did. This fabled stash became known as Yamashita's Treasure...

WHO WAS YAMASHITA?

The Japanese troops were led by General Tomoyuki Yamashita. He was captured by the US at the end of the war, so was never able to retrieve his stolen treasure. Hanged as punishment for his war crimes, the secret location of the treasure died with him... or did it?

General Yamashita pictured at the end of the war

HUNTING FOR RICHES

Rogelio Roxas, a Filipino soldier who served in the army around 20 years after the war, heard stories about the treasure from people connected to General Yamashita. One of them even claimed to have seen a map showing the treasure's location. In 1970, Roxas and a group of fellow treasure hunters began digging in an old mine shaft where they believed the treasure had been hidden. After seven months of backbreaking work, they claimed to have uncovered the secret tunnels where the treasure was stored.

HUGE TREASURE

According to Roxas, the treasure included many gold bars and a solid gold Buddha statue estimated to weigh one ton. When Roxas took the statue back to his house, he discovered that its head could be removed and it had uncut diamonds stashed inside.

An artistic impression of what Roxas claimed he found

STOLEN?

Roxas reported that he tried to sell the Buddha statue, but while he was negotiating a deal, a gang of men wearing army uniforms stormed his house and stole all the riches. Allegedly, it was the Philippine president, Ferdinand Marcos, who ordered the raid. Fearing for his life, Roxas and his family went into hiding, but he was later captured, imprisoned, and tortured—perhaps to silence him about the theft, get him to reveal the treasure's location, or to stop him from going back to the tunnels to claim the rest of the gold.

This image shows the statue that was eventually returned to Roxas' family members, but it was made of bronze and lead, not gold, and they claim it is not the original one found by Roxas.

If the rumors are true, the treasure could be worth billions of dollars. But many think that Yamashita's lost gold is just a legend, fueled by those who dream of digging up a fortune.

WHERE IS THE GOLD NOW?

After ruling as a cruel dictator for years, Ferdinand Marcos (far right) and his family were exiled from the Philippines in 1986. Though Marcos has since died, his widow Imelda (right) has claimed that the president did have Yamashita's legendary gold, but she refuses to say where it is hidden now. There are rumors that he might have had 7,000 tons of gold and that some of it might be concealed in the walls of his house. Perhaps one day a new treasure hunter will track it down.

BLUE LAVA

Molten lava is known for being a fiery red or orange, so if you visit the Kawah Ijen volcano in Indonesia, you might be surprised to see the volcano spewing out what looks like blue lava. But all is not what it seems...

FAMOUS FLAMES

It turns out that the breathtaking blue isn't lava at all! It is fire. Scientists have discovered that sulfur is escaping from inside the volcano. When the sulfur comes in contact with the air and the extreme heat of the lava, it is set on fire and burns with a blue flame. Some of the sulfur is in liquid form, so it oozes down the volcano's slopes as it burns, looking just like lava.

TOXIC

Though this extraordinary volcano may look beautiful, the sulfuric gases stink of rotten eggs and are toxic. Breathing them in can damage your lungs, and they will even make your skin peel. So it might be wise to keep your distance!

SOLVED

Though seeing so much "blue lava" streaming out of a volcano is rare, it can also be seen at the Dallol volcano in Ethiopia, Africa.

The amazing blue flames (right) are only visible at night. In daytime, the lava looks the same as on any other volcano.

This aerial image of Kawah Ijen volcano shows smoke billowing out from its crater.

THE GATE TO HELL

Since ancient times, visitors have flocked to the warm, turquoise pools of Pamukkale in southwest Turkey. Hundreds of these pools cascade down the hillsides, each surrounded by gleaming white limestone. In Roman times, the nearby spa town of Hierapolis was packed with visitors hoping to bathe in the waters, while trying to avoid another more mysterious—and more sinister—location nearby: the Gate to Hell.

MINERAL MOUNTAIN

The otherworldly landscape of Pamukkale is caused by thermal springs. Over thousands of years, mineral-rich water has slowly dripped down the hillside. As the water has evaporated, limestone has been left behind forming a series of snowy white platforms (below). Pamukkale means "Cotton Castle" in Turkish.

TOXIC DOG BREATH

According to Roman myth, Hierapolis was the site of an entrance to the underworld, where the poisonous breath of the three-headed dog Cerberus leaked out into the world, killing anything it touched. A sacred shrine to the god Pluto had been built over this spot. Priests would bring sacrificial animals there, which would drop down dead when they entered the shrine, while the priests mysteriously remained unharmed...

SOLVED

TRUTH BEHIND THE MYTH

Modern scientists wanted to find out if the "Gate to Hell" could really kill animals. The discovered that the air in the shrine contains a high level of carbon dioxide – a very toxic gas. But the carbon dioxide stays low down near the ground. That was why animals died but the humans, who were breathing the clean air higher up, were fine. The gas was released by a volcanic vent, not by a giant, three-headed dog!

The ruins of Hierapolis

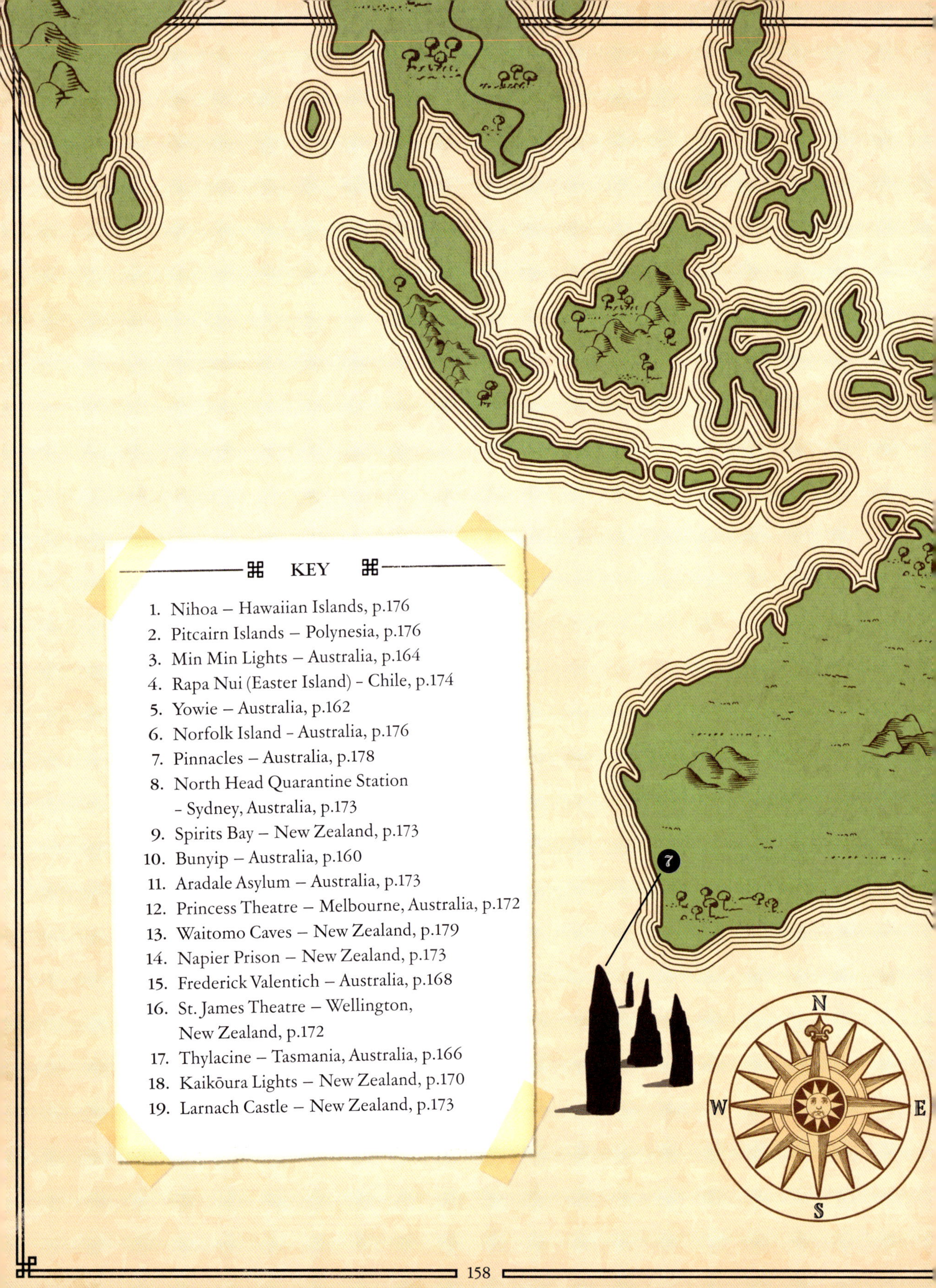

KEY
1. Nihoa – Hawaiian Islands, p.176
2. Pitcairn Islands – Polynesia, p.176
3. Min Min Lights – Australia, p.164
4. Rapa Nui (Easter Island) - Chile, p.174
5. Yowie – Australia, p.162
6. Norfolk Island - Australia, p.176
7. Pinnacles – Australia, p.178
8. North Head Quarantine Station – Sydney, Australia, p.173
9. Spirits Bay – New Zealand, p.173
10. Bunyip – Australia, p.160
11. Aradale Asylum – Australia, p.173
12. Princess Theatre – Melbourne, Australia, p.172
13. Waitomo Caves – New Zealand, p.179
14. Napier Prison – New Zealand, p.173
15. Frederick Valentich – Australia, p.168
16. St. James Theatre – Wellington, New Zealand, p.172
17. Thylacine – Tasmania, Australia, p.166
18. Kaikōura Lights – New Zealand, p.170
19. Larnach Castle – New Zealand, p.173
7
N
W
E
S

OCEANIA

Take a trip around the vast region of Oceania and you'll find the shining cities and baking dry outback of Australia, the wet and wild mountains of New Zealand and the tropical beaches of the many small islands scattered across the Pacific Ocean. But could you also find Australia's monstrous, swamp-dwelling Bunyip or its mysterious Yowie ape-man? If you stick around long enough, you may get a glimpse of the strange Min Min lights or spot a UFO. In this southern continent, there's a mystery around every corner...

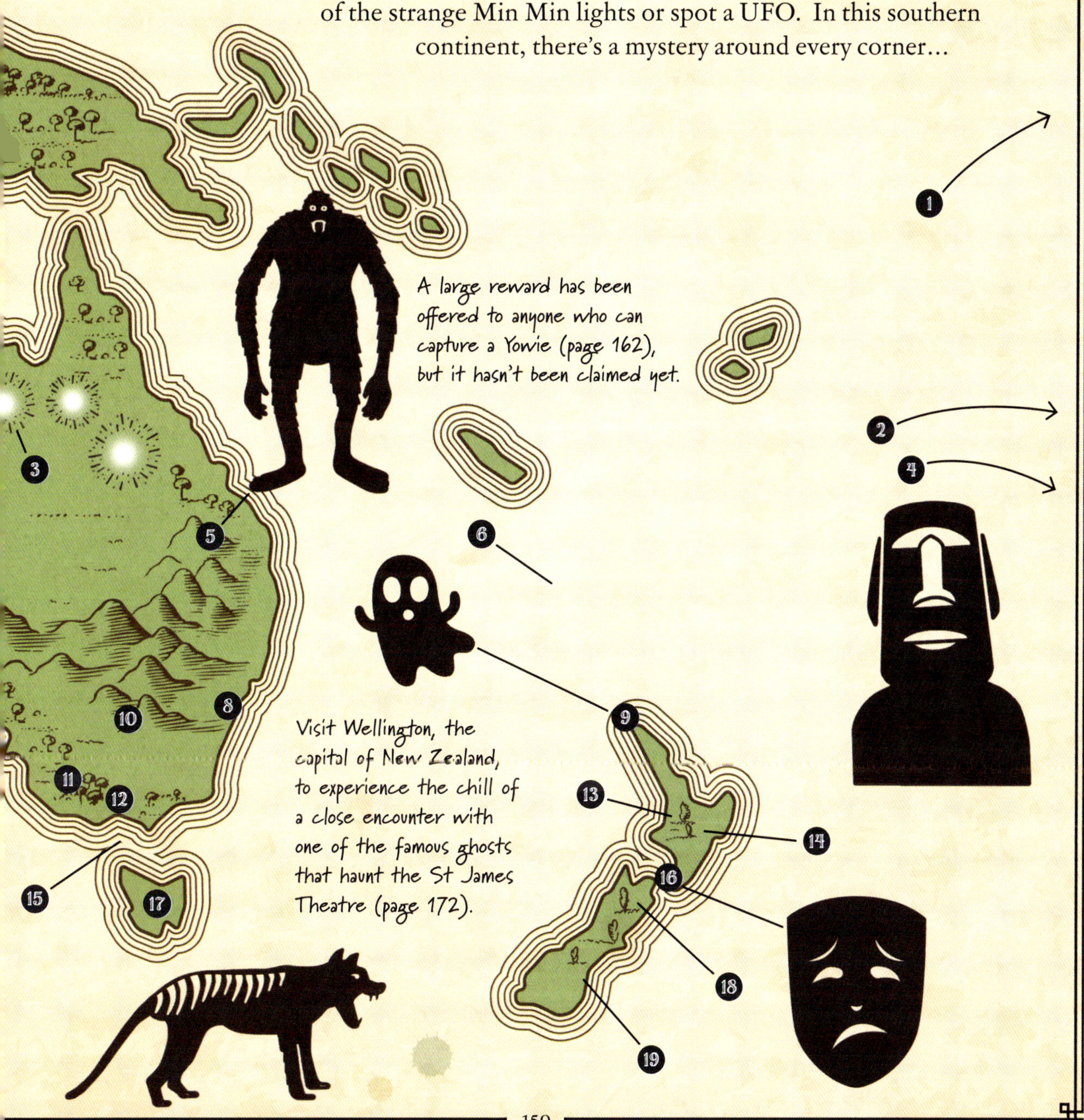

THE BUNYIP

Aboriginal Australian folklore tells of a beast that lurks in the rivers, lakes, and swamps of Australia, waiting to gobble up unsuspecting humans. At night, its booming cry echoes across the outback, sending a shiver through anyone who hears it. So, if you stray into the bush at night, be careful not to linger near the water's edge, or the Bunyip might get you...

What is a Bunyip?

- A large, amphibious animal
- It eats crayfish but will also attack people.
- It lives in water by day and comes onto land to hunt at night.
- It has flippers, which are also said to change into legs when on land.
- It has two large, sharp tusks.
- It has a round, dog-like head.
- It has whiskers like a seal or otter.
- It is about the size of a calf or small cow.
- It is sometimes described as having shaggy fur and a mane, but occasionally said to have scaly skin or feathers.
- It lays eggs in platypus nests.

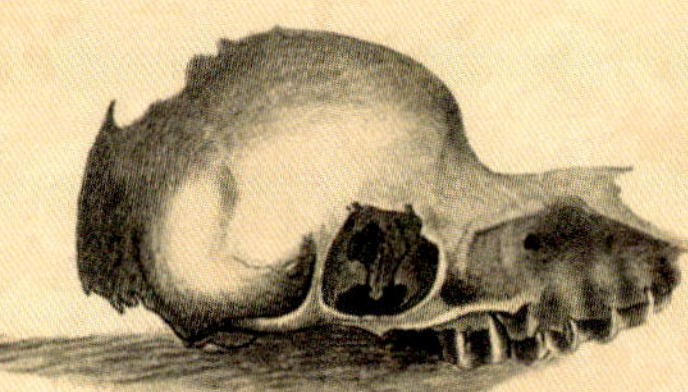

BUNYIP BONES

In 1845, a newspaper article announced that fossil bones had been found, which an Aboriginal Australian had identified as belonging to a Bunyip. The next year, a strange skull thought to be that of a Bunyip was found on the banks of a river (shown in the illustration above). It was put on display at the Australian Museum in Sydney. Unfortunately, experts examining the skull decided it was probably the deformed skull of a baby horse or cow.

MEAT OR VEG?

Aboriginal Australians told European settlers about the Bunyip. As these tales were passed down through the centuries, the creature seems to have become less fearsome. It is now often described as a placid vegetarian, munching on leaves instead of people.

WHAT COULD IT BE?

A SEAL?

In Australia, seals and sea lions are rarely seen away from the coast. But, occasionally, one may stray upriver. It's thought that sightings of such animals could have led to descriptions of a strange and unknown beast. Seals match the Bunyip descriptions in many ways, and they can also make a loud, bellowing noise.

A BIRD'S CALL?

Some people have suggested that the booming cry of the Bunyip could actually be the call of an Australasian bittern, nicknamed the bunyip bird! These birds live in wetlands, but they are secretive and rarely seen.

AN ANCIENT MARSUPIAL?

Diprotodon was a large, grazing marsupial that looked a bit like a giant wombat and lived in Australia until it was wiped out about 46,000 years ago. It was the size of a hippo, with two sharp front teeth that could be mistaken for tusks, but it lived on land, not in water. Perhaps the legend of the Bunyip was passed down and exaggerated over thousands of years, by people who had once seen the *Diprotodon* or its fossilized bones.

A WARNING?

Some people think that tales of the Bunyip were simply told as a way to remind people of the dangers of rivers, lakes, and swamps. If a young child wandered off toward the water, they could all too easily be snatched by a crocodile or sucked down by boggy mud.

THE YOWIE

America has Bigfoot and Asia has the Yeti. Not to be left out, Australia is also said to have its own wild ape man on the loose: the Yowie. But is this cryptid fact or fiction? Well, since Australia has large areas of wilderness where people barely venture, there is plenty of space for a shy creature to stay hidden away...

WHAT DOES IT LOOK LIKE?

The Yowie is said to be covered in hair, sometimes with two pointy teeth poking out of its mouth. In some descriptions it's very large—up to 12 ft. (3.7 m) tall—while in others, it's human-sized. Its arms are long compared to the rest of its body, and it is said to have thick eyebrow ridges and no chin, much like our early human ancestors. There have been sightings of the creature across Australia, but the majority have been in Queensland and New South Wales.

YOWIE HUNTER

Many people are convinced that the Yowie exists. One Yowie Hunter, Rex Gilroy, claimed to have encountered the cryptid on numerous occasions. Pictured here holding what he claimed were casts of the Yowie's footprints, he said, "It was about 5–6 ft (1.5–1.8 m) in height, covered in long, dark hair, and moved upright upon two legs with a stooped gait."

SETTLERS GET A SURPRISE

From almost as soon as European settlers arrived on Australian shores in the late 18th century, there are reported sightings of what would become known as the Yowie. The first known sighting was near Sydney Cove in 1795. Sightings spread across Australia during the 19th century and continue to this day.

WHAT COULD IT BE?

ANCIENT STORIES

There are many figures similar to the Yowie in the traditional stories of Aboriginal Australians. These include the Yaroma, which resembles a large man with hair all over its body (right), hairy little creatures known as Junjudees, and the Dulagarl, a giant figure said to be able to fly (and that eats people). When European settlers came to Australia, they may have heard stories from the Aboriginal peoples and blended them with their own European folklore about wild men of the woods to create a new cryptid.

KANGAROO?

Apart from humans, no other primates live in Australia, so Yowie sightings of the past are unlikely to have been gorillas or chimpanzees. However, some sightings may have actually been kangaroos, which could perhaps at a distance or in poor light be mistaken for a hairy, man-like creature.

WILD MAN?

Other sightings of the Yowie may have been of people who had been living on their own, out in the Australian bush, and had become wild-looking, with overgrown hair.

HOAX OR REALITY?

Just like the Yowie's famous American cousin, some of the Yowie sightings could have been hoaxes, or even people simply making up stories about seeing a strange creature in the bush. Or maybe the stories are true and there's something out there. It's exciting to think that something strange might be in the wilderness, and that you could be the one to find it.

THE MIN MIN LIGHTS

Travel through the Australian outback at night and you might just be lucky—or unlucky—enough to glimpse the spooky Min Min lights. These mysterious illuminations are said to appear floating on the horizon. Sometimes they seem to follow travelers, coming toward them and then vanishing. There are Aboriginal Australian tales of the lights from way back before European settlers came to Australia but, to this day, no one knows what causes them.

EYEWITNESS REPORTS

Though the lights are often described as white, they can also be orange, yellow, blue, green, or red. Some witnesses report that the lights change color as they watch them. They are usually fuzzy and round, and can appear dim or bright, big or small.

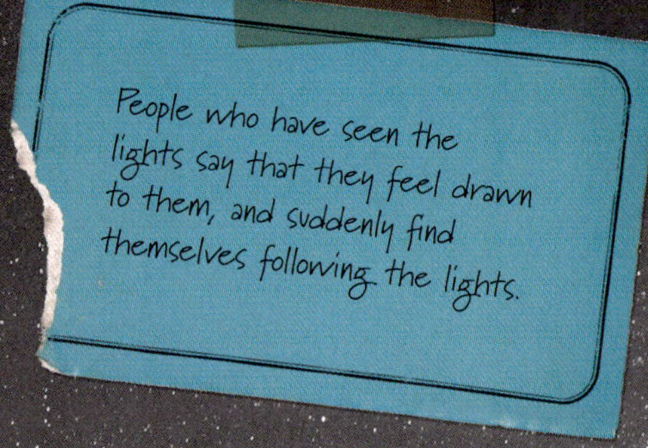

People who have seen the lights say that they feel drawn to them, and suddenly find themselves following the lights.

Even though the lights haven't hurt them, many people report feeling frightened when they catch sight of the freaky phenomenon.

A Queensland sign informing visitors of the Min Min Lights

WHERE TO SEE THEM?

Although there have been sightings of the Min Min lights across Australia, they are most commonly seen in a large, flat area of Queensland known as Channel Country. There was once a town here called Min Min, from which the lights got their name.

WHAT COULD IT BE?

A LOAD OF HOT AIR?

One possible explanation for the lights is that they are a kind of mirage, caused by warm and cold air meeting. This can sometimes reflect lights from below the horizon so that they are visible up in the sky. Aboriginal stories tell of the Min Min lights appearing to stay still, while modern accounts often say they move. This might be because in the past the lights were mirages made by campfires, while today they are made by car headlights (right).

GLOW BUGS?

It has been suggested that the lights could be caused by swarms of bioluminescent insects. Although there are some insects that produce light, there's no evidence of them where Min Min lights have been spotted, and it's unlikely they could produce lights bright enough to be seen on the horizon.

FUNGI?

Another natural solution could be fungi. Australia is home to the *Omphalotus nidiformis*, or ghost fungus. By day, it looks like a normal mushroom but by night it glows with an eerie green light. However, the fungus is mainly found in the south of Australia, not in the area where the Min Min lights have been spotted.

WILL-O'-THE-WISP?

In some places across the world, gases given off by marshy ground are known to produce strange lights. In folktales, these have been called will-o'-the-wisps, jack-o'-lanterns, or spook-lights. They were said to be made by fairies or sprites, as shown in this 19th-century illustration. Could some of the Min Min lights be caused by gases too?

SEARCHING FOR THE THYLACINE

So far, none of the cryptids in this book has been proven to exist. After all, that's what makes them cryptids! But there is one very real animal that has captured the imagination of cryptozoologists across the world: the thylacine. While, officially, the last thylacine died in a zoo in 1936, some believers are hunting for evidence that this animal lives on in the wilds of Australia.

The thylacine is also known as a Tasmanian tiger or Tasmanian wolf. In fact, it wasn't a wolf or a tiger. It was a type of meat-eating marsupial.

SHRINKING TERRITORY

Like most other marsupials, thylacines evolved in Australia. It is thought that the thylacine had died out on mainland Australia by around 3,200 years ago, probably due to climate change, human interference, and because a type of dog called a dingo had arrived on the continent. Luckily, dingoes never reached the Australian island of Tasmania, where the thylacine continued to thrive.

EXTINCT

Unfortunately, the thylacine's troubles weren't over. From the 1800s, European settlers on Tasmania thought that the animal would attack their livestock, and so they hunted it. The animals also faced habitat loss, disease, and being captured for zoos. By the time people realized thylacines were on the brink of extinction, it was too late. No living thylacines were seen after the 1930s and, in 1986, the animal was declared extinct.

A photograph of a pair of thylacines in the National Zoo, Washington D.C., in around 1904

OR IS IT?

Nearly a century since the last known member of the species died, some people are convinced that they have glimpsed the marsupial hiding out in Tasmania's ancient forests (right). Between 1910 and 2019, more than 1,200 alleged sightings were recorded. There have been many expeditions to search for the thylacine but all have come back empty-handed… so far.

OTHER CONTENDERS

Some researchers in Tasmania think that some of the animals survived until at least the 1990s and that there might still be a few left in remote parts of the island. However, others don't think this is likely and that many sightings were simply of dogs or wallabies, or possibly another carnivorous marsupial that did manage to survive, the Tasmanian devil (left).

SUCCESS STORY

Cryptozoologists searching for living thylacines can take hope from the story of the Australian night parrot, also known as the ghost bird. For much of the 20th century, this bird was thought to be extinct. But then a dead night parrot was found in 1990, and finally a live parrot was photographed in 2013. Since then, more have been discovered. Though very rare, the ghost bird lives on. Could the thyalicine be doing the same somewhere?

This is an illustration of a pair of night parrots from the early 19th century. Photos of the bird are still very rare.

DE-EXTINCTION

Though we haven't yet found evidence of thylacines hiding out in the Tasmanian wilderness, some scientists plan to revive the animal in another way. They are hoping to use DNA cloning to create new thylacines in the future. Would you like to see this mysterious animal brought back to life?

THE DISAPPEARANCE OF FREDERICK VALENTICH

In October 1978, a young Australian pilot took his small aircraft on what should have been a short flight. But up in the air, things suddenly turned strange. The pilot, Fred Valentich, radioed ground control to say he was being followed by strange lights. His plane's engine was in trouble. Then there was silence. Valentich and his plane were never seen again.

WHO WAS FRED VALENTICH?

Frederick Valentich, known as Fred, was a 20-year-old pilot. With only 150 hours of flying experience, he still had a long way to go. Fred was said to be a firm believer in UFOs and was worried about being attacked by one. Could that have made him more likely to assume the unexplained lights were from a UFO?

October 21, 6:19 p.m. — Fred takes off from Victoria, Australia. He is heading for King Island.

7:06 p.m. — Fred radios Melbourne Air Flight Service, asking if there are any aircraft flying nearby. He says he can see four strange, bright lights about 1,000 ft. (300 m) above him. He says he is having engine trouble.

7:12 p.m. — There is an unidentified noise, and radio contact is lost.

October 25 — The widespread land, sea, and air search for Valentich's plane is called off, with no trace found.

"It is four bright... it seems to me like landing lights."

"He's playing some sort of game. He's flying over me two, three times."

"As it's flying past, it's a long shape."

"It seems like it's stationary... the thing is just orbiting on top of me."

"It's got a green light and sort of metallic ... it's all shiny ... it just vanished."

"It is hovering, and it's not an aircraft."

—Valentich's description of the UFO

WHY WAS HE FLYING?

Valentich had told some people that he was flying to pick up friends, and others that he was picking up crayfish. However, both these reasons were untrue, and the real reason why he decided to fly the plane that night remains a mystery.

WHAT COULD HAVE HAPPENED?

This reconstruction shows how the four lights may have confused Valentich.

PLANETS?

Some experts think the four lights Valentich saw may have been the planets Venus, Mercury and Mars, and the bright star Antares (below). These would have been visible at that time and place. Since Valentich was so interested in UFOs, he may have seen the seemingly strange lights and jumped to conclusions, panicking and causing the plane to crash.

FATAL ACCIDENT?

Valentich (above) was an inexperienced pilot. He may have become disorientated and flown upside down, mistaking the reflection of his own lights on the water for a spacecraft above him. His plane's engine couldn't have coped with flying upside down for long, and he would have crashed into the sea. Or he may have accidentally put his plane into a downward "graveyard spiral."

ABDUCTED BY ALIENS?

According to some UFOlogists, Valentich's account of the unidentified craft with strange lights following him, as well as eyewitness reports of a green light in the sky, point to an alien abduction. Could Valentich have strayed into the path of a UFO, causing it to capture him and his plane?

FAKED HIS OWN DEATH?

Some think that Valentich actually faked his own disappearance. With enough fuel to fly 500 miles (800 km), Valentich could have traveled far from the search area. But if the young pilot did fake it all, the mystery still remains—why would he do that?

THE KAIKOURA LIGHTS

When someone claims to have seen a UFO, it can be hard to believe they aren't mistaken—or simply making it up. But what if lots of people all see the same thing, and it's caught on camera and radar? Well, then, that's when a mystery gets really intriguing…

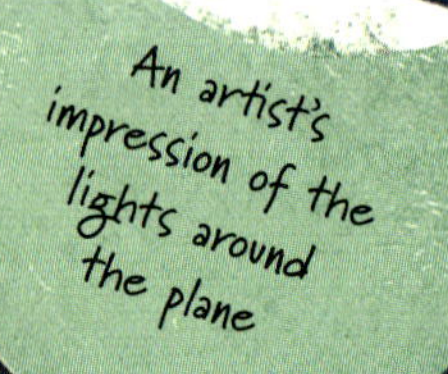

An artist's impression of the lights around the plane

LIGHTS IN THE SKY

In December 1978, the crew of a cargo plane flying over the Kaikōura mountain range in New Zealand spotted five strange lights hovering around their aircraft. The crew claimed the lights kept pace with the plane for several minutes before vanishing and reappearing in a different place.

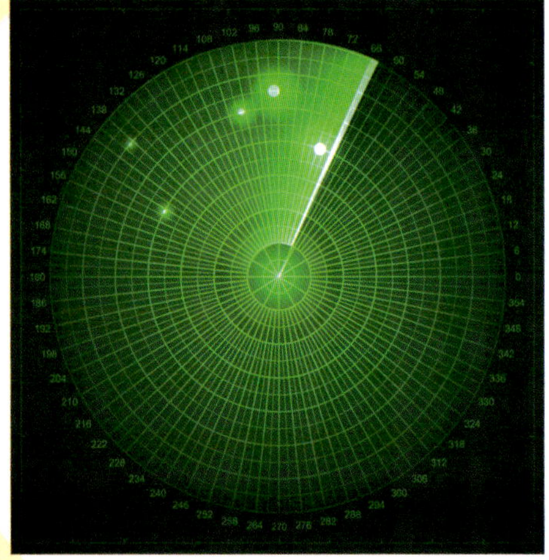

RADAR RECORD

A week later, a television crew came aboard the cargo plane and filmed the unidentified lights. They reported that one of the objects even followed the airplane until just before it landed. The airplane took off again, and the crew saw what was described as a large, lighted orb around 2,000 ft. (600 m) away. It was filmed keeping pace with the plane for about 15 minutes. What's more, the lights appeared as unidentified objects on the radar systems of both the airplane and air traffic control.

Since these first sightings, there have been occasional reports of people seeing strange lights around the same area. The last time this happened was in 2015.

WHAT COULD THE LIGHTS BE?

OPTICAL ILLUSION?

New Zealand's Ministry of Defence (MOD) thought that the lights may have been from fishing boats, trains, or cars that were reflecting off clouds, making it appear as though the lights were in the sky. There are also natural phenomena known as subsuns and sundogs (right), which are caused by sunlight being bent by ice crystals in clouds to create what look like glowing globes of light. Could something similar have happened at night but with artificial lights?

PLANETS OR SHOOTING STARS?

The MOD also suggested that the lights may have been meteors or the planet Venus, which can sometimes look very bright in the night sky. But planets don't move, and meteors usually burn out in just a few seconds, so those explanations seem unlikely.

UFOs?

Ufologists dismissed the MOD's explanations. They argued that if the lights were caused by something as common as a fishing boat, why was the official investigation marked as "Top Secret"? They are convinced that the lights were from UFOs, like the one in the artist's impression below.

THE MYSTERY CONTINUES

Perhaps the most puzzling thing about the Kaikōura lights is their appearance on radar systems. If they were indeed simply Venus or an unusual optical illusion caused by lights on the ground, then what were the moving objects showing up on the radar? Those hoping for answers keep watching the Kaikōura mountains, hoping that one day the strange wandering lights will return…

HAUNTED OCEANIA

There are many spine-tingling tales of ghosts haunting historic buildings across Australia and New Zealand. From theaters and prisons to hospitals and castles, there seems to be no shortage of places where restless spirits can leave their imprint on this continent.

STAGE FRIGHT

If you visit the St. James Theatre in Wellington, New Zealand, you might get more drama than you paid for! This historic theater, built in 1912, is said to be the haunt of several ghosts.

The theater's most famous phantom is the ghost of a Russian dancer called Yuri, who fell to his death from the theater's rigging. Yuri is a friendly ghost who plays with the stage lights at the end of the night. He is said to have even saved the life of a projectionist by pushing him out of the way of a falling beam.

A less helpful ghost is the Wailing Woman, who is often heard moaning at night. She is said to have been a struggling actress, distressed at being booed off stage. Now she causes accidents in the theater as revenge for how she was treated.

ACTORLY APPARITION

Australia has its own haunted theater, the Princess Theatre in Melbourne. The ghost of actor Frederick Federici (below) is said to have roamed the playhouse since he died of a heart attack while on stage. He's more of a friendly mascot than a scary specter, though. He even has his own seat left empty for every opening performance so that he can enjoy the show.

There are claims that a boys' choir has been heard singing at the St. James Theatre. The haunting tunes are thought to come from a group lost at sea during World War II. They had performed their final show at the theater.

ARADALE ASYLUM

This huge hospital, which was once used for treating people with mental illness, is now a college. With many reports of ghosts and paranormal activity, it is one of Australia's most haunted buildings.

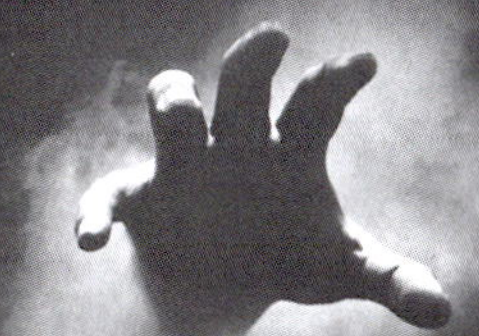

OTHER HAUNTED PLACES

Larnach Castle, Dunedin, New Zealand – Built in 1871, this stately home was the site of many sad deaths. The ghost of the owner's daughter, Katie, is said to be seen dancing around the grand ballroom.

Napier Prison, Napier, New Zealand – New Zealand's oldest prison is said to be haunted by an infamous mass-murderer. People have also reported hearing strange footsteps and seeing doors open and close on their own. The former jail is now open to tourists, so you can go ghost-hunting yourself… if you're feeling brave enough!

North Head Quarantine Station, Sydney, Australia – For over 150 years, people suspected of having an infectious disease were held at this isolated compound. With hundreds dying and being buried on the site, it's no surprise that many ghostly apparitions have been observed here.

Spirits Bay, New Zealand – Ghosts don't just dwell in old buildings. On the northern tip of New Zealand lies a sandy beach known as Spirits Bay or Piwhane. This bay is sacred to the Māori. Legend has it that spirits of the dead gather at an old tree above the bay, before traveling down to the water to return to their homeland, the afterlife.

THE GIANT HEADS OF RAPA NUI

Far out in the Pacific Ocean, west of South America, lies Rapa Nui, also known as Easter Island. There, against a bare, grassy landscape, stand hundreds of massive stone statues. For centuries, people have pondered the reasons why they were made and how a group of ancient islanders could have ever moved such heavy statues into place.

WHAT ARE THE STONE HEADS?

The impressive statues, known as *moai* (pronounced *mo-eye*), were carved between 1100 and 1680 CE. Most of the 887 statues are around 13 ft. (4 m) tall and weigh around 15 tons. There is evidence that the moai's eyes were once made from white coral and shiny black obsidian, like this one on the left.

ISOLATED ISLAND

Rapa Nui is more than 600 miles (1,000 km) away from any other inhabited island. The language and the people of the island are also known as Rapa Nui. It's thought that Polynesians discovered the tiny island by around 1000 CE, but experts aren't sure which island they originally came from and whether they came on purpose or by accident.

UP TO THEIR NECKS

It might seem at first glance like many of the Easter Island statues are giant heads. In fact, they have torsos too. Over time, these have been buried underground. Archaeologists have uncovered some of these figures, as shown in this photograph.

HONORING THE ANCESTORS

Archaeologists have found burial sites at the base of the statues, suggesting that families buried their dead with the statue of their ancestor. It is thought that the moai were made to honor the islander's ancestors or possibly their chiefs and other important elders, but we may never know for sure. Almost all the original Rapa Nui either died or left the island in a very short space of time once Europeans came to the island. This meant that much of the cultural knowledge passed down through the generations was lost.

HOW WERE THE MOAI MOVED?

Archaeologists aren't sure how the immense moai statues were moved from the quarry to their final positions. Some think they may have been tugged by ropes, "walking" the statues forward with a rocking motion. Others suggest they might have been attached to a kind of wooden sled and rolled across tree trunks, pulled along by hundreds of men. Most of the island's trees were cut down by the Rapa Nui. Could they have been using them to move the statues?

This image shows how the remaining moai stand in lines with their backs to the sea, watching over the island.

THE QUARRY

The Rapa Nui got the stone for their moai statues from a quarry. Incredibly, around 400 of the moai statues were never completed or moved, and they can still be found at the quarry today. Most of the moai were made from tuff, a soft rock from volcanic ash that is easy to carve.

IN DANGER

There is still so much we don't know about these incredible sculptures. Unfortunately, they are in danger of being destroyed before we can find out more answers. In 2022, a wildfire damaged hundreds of the moai, while rising sea levels also threaten the many statues that stand near the coast.

THE MYSTERY ISLANDS

Many islands are scattered across the vast Pacific Ocean. For a thousand years or more, most have been home to thriving communities. But the Mystery Islands are different. In the 16th and 17th centuries, when European sailors began to explore some of the tiniest, most remote islands, they found them empty of people. You might think that humans had never set foot there before, but archaeologists have now found clues that people did once live on these islands. So what could have happened to these ancient islanders?

SKILLED SEAFARERS

Polynesian islanders were skilled seafarers and navigators, able to travel thousands of miles across the ocean in canoes, guided by the stars. Their voyages likely took weeks or months, but by 1250 CE, they had settled on islands as distant as New Zealand in the south, Rapa Nui (Easter Island) in the east, and Hawaii in the north.

A modern replica of a double-hulled canoe of the type the Polynesians used on their voyages of discovery

WHERE ARE THE MYSTERY ISLANDS?

At least 12 islands have been found to have once been home to humans, then later abandoned. They are spread out across Polynesia, in some of the most remote parts of the Pacific Ocean. Among them are Norfolk Island (near New Zealand), Nihoa (near Hawaii), and the Pitcairn Islands in the southern Pacific Ocean.

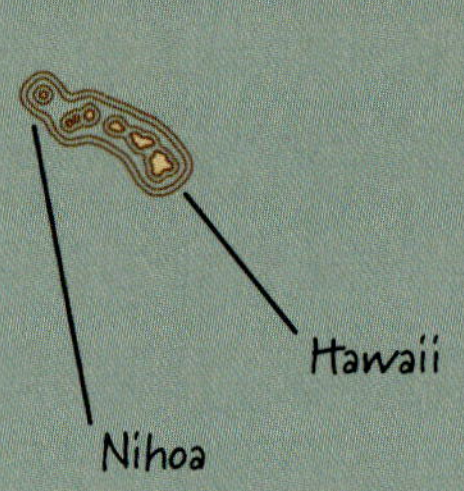

Pitcairn Islands

Rapa Nui

Norfolk Island

Archaeological finds, including stone and ivory tools, show that people lived on islands such as Norfolk Island for more than 200 years before disappearing.

WHAT COULD HAVE HAPPENED?

NATURAL DISASTER?

No one is sure what caused the Polynesian Mystery Islands to be deserted, and there may well have been more than a single factor. Perhaps each island has its own story to tell—if only it could speak. But what is certain is that on such small, remote islands, natural disasters such as a drought, wildfire, or tsunami could have had a devastating impact.

HABITAT DAMAGE?

Perhaps the Polynesian settlers damaged the island ecosystems, leading to a shortage of food and natural resources. They may have cut down too many trees to build homes and boats, and to make room for planting crops such as bananas. Rats that hitched a ride with the Polynesian settlers may have also threatened native species.

Polynesian rats spread right across the region as stowaways on boats.

THIRST AND HUNGER?

It's possible that the islands were too small to support the growing populations. Archaeologists think that on many of the islands, humans may have relied on hunting birds for food, many of which then went extinct. On some islands, there may not have been enough fresh drinking water available.

WAR AND SICKNESS?

If food, water, and other natural resources were limited, the islanders may have ended up fighting one another, with some being killed or leaving to find new lands. Alternatively, the interactions between the islands may have been peaceful, but these small isolated communities may have struggled to cope with unfamiliar diseases brought to them by visitors from far away.

LONELINESS?

The Mystery Islands are hundreds or thousands of miles from any other land. It's possible that the communities living on them felt too isolated and wanted to return to the homeland of their ancestors.

Life would have been lonely on Pitcairn Island, over 370 miles (600 km) from its nearest neighbor.

THE PINNACLES

Once mistaken for the remains of an ancient city, these spectacular skyscraper rocks rise up out of the desert in Western Australia. Geologists are still trying to unpick exactly how these thousands of mysterious pillars were formed.

WHAT ARE THEY?

The Pinnacles are a collection of several thousand rocks poking up through the desert floor. Some are tall and spiky, while others have worn away into shapes that resemble tombstones and mushrooms. The biggest are up to 12 ft. (3.5 m) high.

FOSSILIZED GHOSTS

The structures have long been known to the Aboriginal peoples of the region, the Noongar. According to one tradition, the place was sacred to women but, long ago, some men walked through the area. As a punishment, the gods buried them alive. The pinnacles are what remain of their weapons, held up to the gods in a plea for forgiveness.

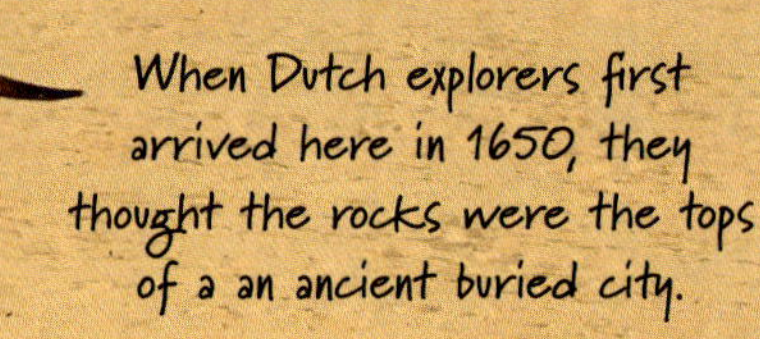

MYSTERY SOLVED... OR IS IT?

We now know the Pinnacles are a natural feature, thought to have formed around 30,000 years ago. They are made from limestone rock. As wind and water eroded the sandy soil around them over time, the harder limestone of the Pinnacles remained. However, geologists are still trying to unpick exactly what made the limestone form such strange, pillar-like shapes. One theory is that calcium from the sandy ground collected around plant and tree roots, building up into solid casts over time.

THE GLOWING CAVES

Entering the glowing Waitamo Caves of New Zealand, you would be forgiven for thinking you'd stepped inside a fairy's grotto. But these speckles of glowing blue light scattered across the cave's rocky ceiling aren't magic… they're mucus!

MĀORI DISCOVERY

Long ago, it's said that local people would not set foot in the dark Waitomo Caves, believing the eerily glowing caverns were entrances to the underworld. However, in 1887, a Māori chief called Tane Tinorau became the first person to explore Waitamo, using candlelight to guide him as he floated on a raft along the underground river that flows through the caves.

The caves seem to shimmer with a strange blue light.

SOLVED

WHAT'S CAUSING THE GLOW?

The breathtaking sight is caused by millions of fungus gnat larvae, also known as glowworms. Each larva makes droplets of sticky mucus that hang on thin threads of silk, dangling down from its bioluminescent abdomen. The glowing light attracts tiny prey, such as mayflies, which then are trapped in the mucus. The larva pulls up the sticky silk threads like a fisher with a fishing line, and gobbles up the unfortunate prey.

GROSS GLOW

In 2016, scientists finally figured out what the glowworms' sticky fishing lines are made from. And the answer is… urea, the same substance found in urine! The discovery gets even more gross—while most animals get rid of urea from their rear ends, the glowworm's sticky mucus comes out of its mouth.

ANTARCTICA

Antarctica is so mysterious that, up until around 200 years ago, no one was sure whether it even existed. It wasn't until 1820 that a Russian expedition sailed close enough to catch sight of the continent, and nobody set foot there until 1895. Since then, several weird phenomena have been discovered, including "singing" ice and a glacier that seems to be oozing blood. Despite modern equipment, the ice shelf remains a difficult and dangerous place to explore, but scientists are slowly trying to unravel its secrets.

KEY

1. Third-Man Factor – Shackleton's ship trapped in ice, p.182
2. South Pole
3. Vostok Research Station – Princess Elizabeth Land
4. Singing Ice – Ross Ice Shelf, p.184
5. Snow Chimneys & Lava Lake – Mount Erebus, p.185
6. Blood Falls – Taylor Glacier, McMurdo Dry Valleys, p.184

Only a few thousand people live and work on Antarctica's scientific bases each year. Would you travel to Earth's most isolated—and coldest—continent in search of mystery?

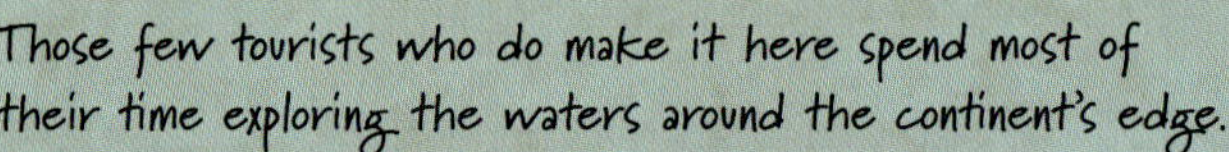

Those few tourists who do make it here spend most of their time exploring the waters around the continent's edge.

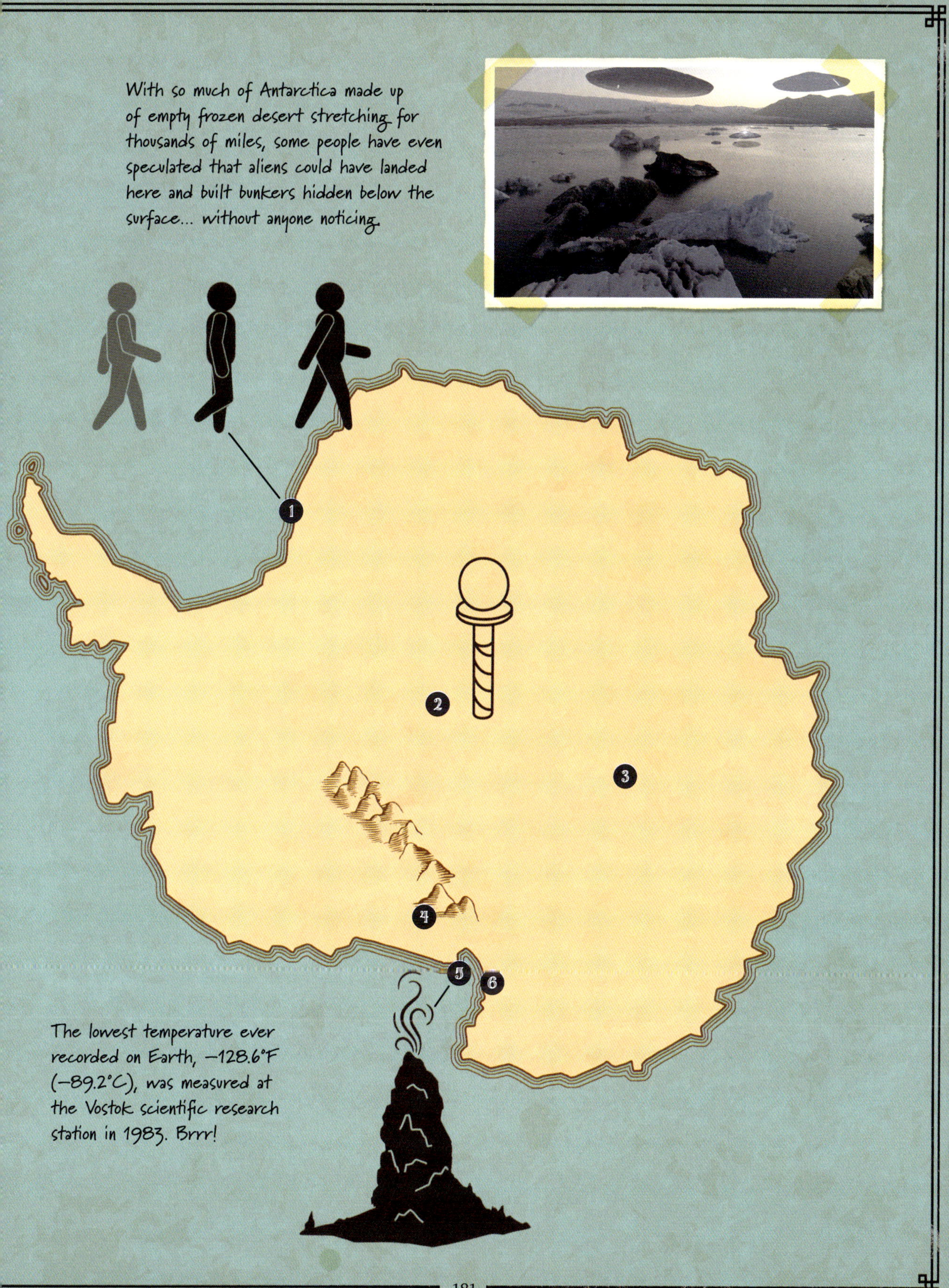
With so much of Antarctica made up of empty frozen desert stretching for thousands of miles, some people have even speculated that aliens could have landed here and built bunkers hidden below the surface... without anyone noticing.
1
2
3
4
5
6
The lowest temperature ever recorded on Earth, −128.6°F (−89.2°C), was measured at the Vostok scientific research station in 1983. Brrr!

THIRD-MAN FACTOR

Antarctica is a land of howling winds and extreme cold. With glistening white ice and snow stretching for thousands of miles, and no other humans around to send help, it is a land that has tested explorers to their limits. In life-or-death moments, a strange and unexplained phenomenon has been experienced, almost like a ghostly presence. It is known as the third-man factor.

INVISIBLE COMPANION

The third-man factor (also known as the third-man syndrome) has been described as the feeling that there is another being with you, and that their presence is helping you in a time of stress or danger, offering comfort and support, or even guidance. This phenomenon isn't just experienced in Antarctica. It has been reported around the world by explorers, mountaineers, astronauts, and others in life-threatening situations.

SHACKLETON'S EXPERIENCE

In 1916, the Anglo-Irish explorer Ernest Shackleton set out on a dangerous and exhausting rescue mission in Antarctica, alongside two companions. Their ship had become stuck in ice and they needed to get help to save the rest of their stranded team. This meant first sailing across 800 miles (1,200 km) of freezing open ocean, then trekking across the mountains of a remote Antarctic island to reach a whaling station. If they failed, everyone would die. On the final trek (right), all three experienced the same weird feeling: that there was another, invisible, person with them.

Shackleton's ship was eventually crushed by the ice.

WHAT COULD IT BE?

A WAY TO COPE?

It might be that when we are in a stressful and dangerous situation, our brain can create the feeling of there being someone else with us, helping us to get to safety. Scientists need to do more research to find out how this might work.

GUARDIAN ANGEL?

Some people think that the "third man" doesn't come from inside our mind at all, and that instead it is a spiritual being, like a guardian angel, that has been sent to help us. Some who have experienced the third-man factor felt that an angel was with them, even if they were not religious.

A HELPING HAND

Some have described the "third man" as an invisible presence—just the feeling that someone else is with them. Others report hearing a voice that guides them to safety. The presence certainly seemed to help Shackleton. He and his companions reached the whaling station, where they were able to get a ship to rescue their stranded comrades. All 27 men on the expedition survived. But was it because they received paranormal assistance?

"I know that during that long and racking march of thirty-six hours over the unnamed mountains and glaciers of South Georgia it seemed to me often that we were four, not three."

—Ernest Shackleton (1874–1922), Antarctic explorer

THE MYSTERY CONTINUES

For now, no one knows for sure what causes the third-man factor. Some people who have spiritual beliefs are certain it is a helpful force such as a guardian angel, while scientists say it is the work of our own minds. Perhaps one day we will know for sure what causes this fascinating—and helpful—phenomenon.

MYSTERY SOLVED!

Antarctica is a land like no other, a vast desolate stretch of snow and ice where human beings have never been able to establish permanent settlements. Nature here sometimes acts in ways that are different from the rest of the world, creating bizarre phenomena that scientists have only recently been able to explain.

BLOOD FALLS

Against a blanket of white, vivid red liquid gushes out of a glacier in East Antarctica like a gruesome flow of blood. What causes this strange sight perplexed scientists for many years. At first, people thought that the creepy color was caused by red algae, but why would the water stay as a liquid, instead of freezing solid like the rest of the glacier?

WHAT CAUSES THE COLOR?

In 2017, scientists solved the mystery by using radar to scan beneath the glacier. They found that underneath the ice is a lake filled with very salty water that is so rich in iron that it has turned red. Salt water stays liquid at much lower temperatures than fresh water, which is why this blood-red water can bubble out from cracks in the glacier.

SINGING ICE

When Antarctic researchers put special sensors out to monitor the ice shelf, they didn't expect to hear the ice "singing." After two years of recording, the scientists discovered that the ice was constantly humming—but the sound was too low for humans to hear. When the sound is played back at a higher pitch that we can hear, it sounds like something ghostly or alien! In fact, it turns out that the sound is made by the ice vibrating as the powerful polar winds sweep over its surface.

SNOW CHIMNEYS

Bizarre-looking structures line the slopes of Mount Erebus, Antarctica's most active volcano. Scientists have discovered that these "snow chimneys" form where hot gases escape from the molten lava inside the volcano. As the gases stream out of the volcano, they turn the snow and ice into billowing steam.

SOLVED

As the steam hits the cold air, it freezes, building up a tall chimney, almost like a mini ice volcano! Some of the snow chimneys reach an impressive 60 ft. (18 m) high.

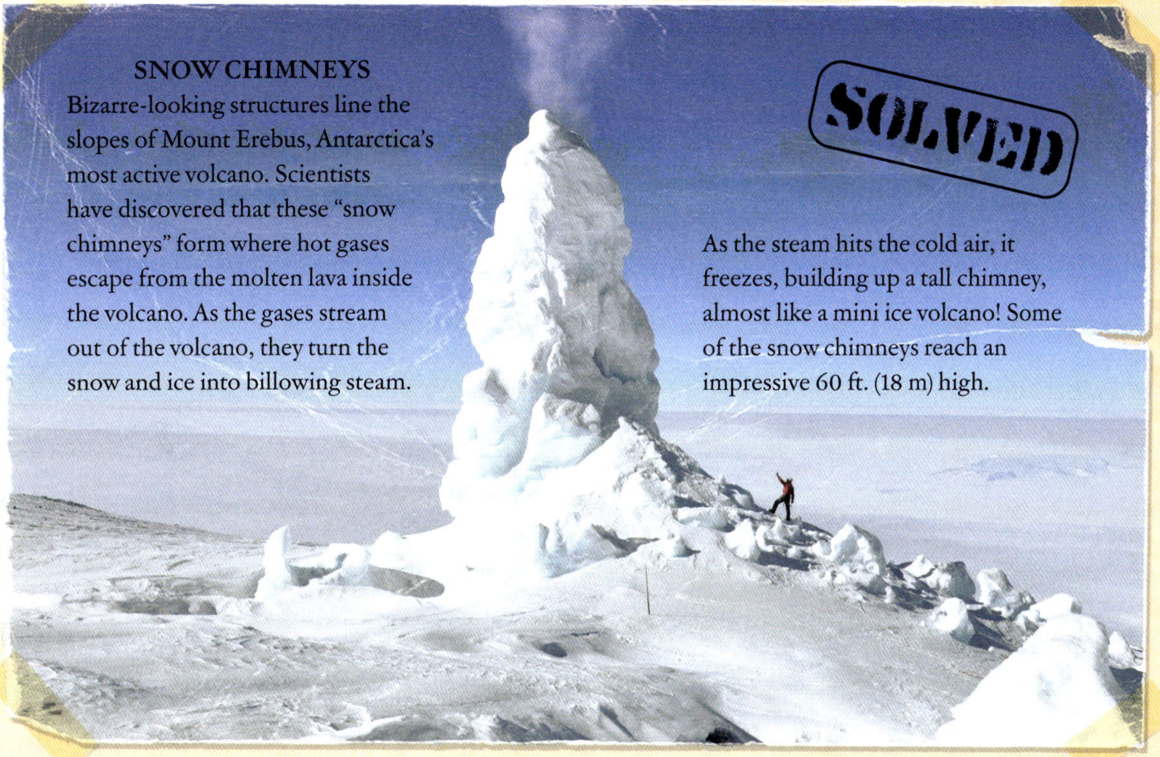

THE LAVA LAKE

The snow chimneys aren't the only incredible thing about Mount Erebus. It may look like it's completely frozen over, but the first people to climb the peak were astonished to find a boiling lake of lava at its summit, which may be 300 ft. (100 m) deep. An observatory has been set up on the volcano so that scientists can research more of its secrets. You'd have to be brave to go there, though—the volcano can spew out huge lava bombs that can land up to 1 mile (1.6 km) away.

A line of smoke from the volcano's summit (above) indicates the presence of the boiling lava lake (left).

DO YOU WANT TO BELIEVE?

So what do you believe? Every corner of the world has a mystery to uncover, but some explanations seem more likely than others. Often stories become more elaborate and fantastic as they are passed from person to person, and it can be hard to track down the grains of truth at their center.

MYTH MAKERS

Throughout history, there have been many things that we have found hard to explain. In the past, people often didn't have the scientific knowledge to be able to figure out the answers, so they made up stories to explain what they saw around them. That's how myths about the aurora borealis (left and page 42), the Blue Grotto (page 88), and the Pinnacles (page 178) began. Perhaps today's mysteries will be solved by science in the future. Or perhaps there are some things that we'll never understand.

CLASH OF CULTURES

Around the world, cultures pass down stories that often contain a message about how to behave or stay safe. This may involve inventing a creature, such as the Bogeyman of Europe, to scare children into doing the right thing. Some claim the Australian Bunyip (left and page 160) has a similar origin. Often, when people have colonised areas, they have heard the stories of the people living there and adapted them, sometimes believing that symbolic monsters were real. We need to be careful to treat the origins of these legends with respect.

PROCEED WITH CAUTION

When it comes to mysteries, people often only see what they want to see. If you're sure aliens have visited Earth, you might be more likely to think you've spotted a UFO. If you believe in ghosts, a chill on the back of your neck might be the sign of a spirit instead of a simple draught. If you don't trust the government, you might think they are covering up the truth. When you read or listen to accounts of the unexplained, try to think critically about who is telling the story and why. Are they telling you all the facts? Is there another side to the story?

KEEP LOOKING

These days, we can catch a plane across the globe, view satellite pictures from space, and livestream from a submersible deep below the ocean's surface. It can feel like there is nothing left to discover, so believing in a mystery can add a bit of magic and adventure to our lives. So, keep your eyes, ears, and mind open. You never know—the next mystery might be solved by you.

GLOSSARY

amphibious Able to live both in water and on land

ancestor A person from whom you are descended

apparition A vision, often thought to be a ghost or spirit

archaeologist A person who uncovers and studies buried structures, objects, and other remains from the past

artifact A human-made object, often something from the past

bioluminescence The ability of a living thing to produce its own light

cannibal A person who eats other humans, or an animal that eats its own kind

civilisation An advanced human society that has government, culture, and often towns, farming, written language, and people who do specialized jobs

colony A group of people who have left their homeland to form a settlement in a different place, sometimes by conquest

conspiracy A secret plot or plan between people, likely with a deceitful, harmful, or illegal aim, that is kept hidden from the general public

conspiracy theorist A person who doesn't believe the accepted explanation for an event and instead thinks that there is a secret plot to keep the truth from the public

cryptid A creature whose existence hasn't been proven

cryptozoology The study of cryptids, including the search for evidence to prove they exist

culture A group of people and their way of life, customs, and beliefs (there have been many different cultures throughout history and around the world)

curse Magic incantation or spell cast to inflict harm or bad luck on another person

extinct Having died out, with no living individuals of a species left anywhere in the world

eyewitness A person who has seen something with their own eyes, rather than just hearing or reading about it

folklore Traditional stories, customs, and beliefs passed down within a community or culture

geoglyph A large drawing or design on the ground, made from earth or stones, or by removing the surface of the ground

habitat A natural environment where a plant or animal lives, such as cacti living in a desert habitat or gorillas living in a tropical rainforest habitat

humanoid A creature that is human-like in shape or characteristics, such as Bigfoot, mermaids, elves, goblins, and some aliens and robots

indigenous Describes the original, earliest-known inhabitants of a land and those who are descended from them

legend A story passed down over time, often claiming to be true but without any hard evidence

myth A traditional story or legend, often involving a supernatural element or used as a way of explaining something, such as the creation of the world (myth can also be used to describe something that is untrue)

phenomenon An event that can be observed—usually something unusual or extraordinary

physical evidence Objects or materials that can be seen or held, such as blood, footprints, and fingerprints

prehistoric From a time in the past, before written human history

pterosaur A prehistoric flying reptile

sarcophagus A stone coffin, often decorated with carvings

sceptic A person who doubts or questions the claims or beliefs of others

settler A person who has moved to a new country or area

Soviet Union A large, communist state that existed from 1922 to 1991, encompassing Russia and many of the surrounding countries

spirit A ghost or other supernatural being without a solid form

spy A person who watches or looks through the belongings of another person or organisation to find out secret information

superstition An irrational belief that isn't based on fact, often to do with the idea that something bad will happen, such as the belief that it is unlucky to break a mirror or for a black cat to cross your path

theory An explanation of facts or events that isn't yet proven

UFO Stands for 'unidentified flying object' and is a term often used to mean an object suspected of being an alien spacecraft

INDEX

CREDITS

The publisher would like to thank the following for their kind permission to reproduce their images

Key: l - left, r - right, t - top, b - bottom, c - center, b/g - background

Shutterstock.com: Merlin74 back cover cl, 53 tr; Kobee endpapers, 34-35, 58-59, 78-79, 128-129; pingebat 4-5, 8-9, 45, 62-63, 90-91, 93, 107, 112-113, 132-133 158-159; Raggedstone 6-7 b/g; andreiuc88 6-7 b/g; Aleksandr Stezhkin 10 tl; Charles Bartley Firth 11 cl; Rodworks 11 cr; Lflorot 12 br; Everett Collection 14 cr; Beautiful landscape 15 cl; Valentina Razumova 15 cr; JM-Media 16 bl, 19 bl, 20-21 b/g, 74-75 b/g, 150 tr; andryuha1981 17 tr; Scott Rothstein 17 bc; CJO Photography 18 br; Danita Delimont 21 tr, 131 br; kamomeen 21 cl; Hatteviden 21 br; Cvandyke 24 bl; Konstantin L 25 b; Jim Larkin 28 br; Steve Lagreca 29 b; patat 32-33, 186-187, 192; Dotted Yeti 32 br; Yvan p36 c; Ronnie Howard 39 tr; Kanokratnok 39 cl; Inspired By Maps 41 t; MarcelClemens 41 cl; Alena Ohneva 41 br; Sean Xu 42 b/g, 186; Qing Ding 43 cr; Prakasit Nuansri 43 c; Simon Pittet 46 br; Allexanderh 48 c; Mauro Rodrigues 49 cr; Teo Tarras 50-51 b/g; Ursatii 53-53 b/g, 78 bl, 95 cr; Fagner Martins 53 br; Dmitry Burlakov 54 cr; adike 54 bl; Damian Ryszawy 55 tr; funstarts33 56-57 b/g; Elif Bayraktar 57 tr; Viagens e Caminhos 57 bl; Miroslav Denes 58-59 b/g; panos3 59 tr; SC Image 59 br; Hatteviden 65 b; 4kclips 67 t; Orest lyzhechka 68 t; Rich Carey 68 b; BlueSnap 69 tl; Dotted Yeti 69 c; Nicholas Grey 70 b/g; Cavan-Images 72-73 b/g; Marc Cid 73 t; Henryk Sadura 72 br b/g; DCProduction Media 72 br; mon69r 74-75 b; Eric Isselee 75 br; Iakov Kalinin 76-77 b/g ; Milan Zygmunt 77 tl; Ondrej Chvatal 77 bl; Daniel Marian 78-79 b/g; salajean 79 tr; Paul Horia Malaianu 79 b; valda butterworth 82-83 b/g; Viacheslav Lopatin 82 tl; Dmytro Pientsov 84-85 b/g; Vicushka 85 t; Heracles Kritikos 85 br; Anda Mikelsone 86 bl; Robert Szymanski 86-87 b.g; alexei_tm 87 tr; Marti Bug Catcher 87 bl; takmat71 88 b/g; ryan7 88 br; Sahara Prince 89 tr; Andrey_Kuzmin 92 cl; EvrenKalinbacak 93 b; Best-Backgrounds 94 tr; Japan's Fireworks 94 cl; Strelyuk 94 br; LIAL 96 tl; norhazlan 96 cr; Mommii287 97 tl; Mark Canning 97 tr; Tomer raiss 97 c; Morphart Creation 98 tl; Tithi Luadthong 102-103 b/g; Sugrit Jiranarak 111 tr; Richard Art Gallary 111 cr; Vlad Siaber 114-115 b/g; DanieleGay 115 tr, 187 cr; givaga 115 cl; Jaroslav Moravcik 116 cl; Sandro Zahra 118 br; Nick Brundle Photography 118 cr; Wayne Marinovich 123 bl; Paco Como 125 cl; Jurgen Vogt 125 cr; Vladimir Turkenich 125 tr; Thomas Retterath 127 cl; Erik Zandboer 127 br; Jan Willem van Hofwegen 129 tr; Patrick Poendl 129 br; Triff 134-135 b/g; buradaki 135 tr; Aureliy 137 tr; Jamo Images 138 tl; Jukka Palm 139 tr; Morphart Creation 139 bl, 139 br; RealityImages 141 cl; Matyas Rehak 142 cr; Iwanami Photos 142-143 b/g; Ed Berlen 143 c; Alice_illustrations 144-145 b/g; PTZ Pictures 146 b/g; Sanga Park 147 br; Warpaint 148 r; Sammy33 149 cl; Zuzana Gabrielova 149 bl; Raggedstone 150-151 b/g; Lubo Ivanko 151 tl; Javi Az 151 cl; Mekong on tour 152 tr; birdbyb stockphoto 152 bl; Traiphop Noiwimol 153 tr; Patrick Foto 153 bl; Mazur Travel 156 c; Putu Artana 156 b/g; Suksamran1985 157 b/g; Nejdet Duzen 157 bl; AndreasM8 161 tr; Imogen Warren 161 cl; zef art 165 tr; Chase D'animulls 165 cl; Petar B photography 165 cr; Kazuki Yamakawa 167 tr; Pozdeyev Vitaly 168-169 b/g; Robert Buchel 169 tl; Brave Behind the Lenz 170 b/g; SkillUp 170 bl; PhotoJanski 171 tr; Nazarii_Neshcherenskyi 171 cl; rangizzz 172-173 b/g; Alfonso Soler 172-172 l & r; Fotokita 173 tl; Nils Versemann 173 tr; GTW 174 cl; ChameleonsEye 178; Shaun Jeffers 179 tr; David Merron Photography 180 b; ImageBank4u 181 tr; vchal 183 rc; Envirosense 185 br ; Multiple pages MaxyM, Scottchan, Carolyn Franks, Alena_D, rangizzz; Shutterstock.AI 6 cl, 19 br, 47 tr, 154 br, 184 bl.

Alamy: Science Photo Library back cover tl, 95 tr, 150 br; gary corbett 14 tl; Robert Hill 15 tr; Matthew Corrigan 16 tr, 38, 150 bl; Design Pics Inc 17 cr; Tom Uhlman 18 tr; Science History Images 22 cr, 22 bl, 76 br, 174 br; North Wind Picture Archives 23 tr; Chronicle 30, 65 cr, 70 cr, 98 c, 99 tr, 105 cl, 125 bl; Charles Walker Collection 31 tr, 31 bl, 162 r; Granger - Historical Picture Archive 31 cl, 71 cl; Carver Mostardi 36 br; Objectum 37 t; United Archives GmbH 39 cr; Daniel Eskridge 39 br; James L. Peacock 40 tr; Flhc Madb1 42 bl; david sanger photography 50 cr; mauritius images GmbH 60, 96 bl; Octavio Campos Salles 61 tr; Pulsar Imagens 61 c; Ian Cowe 64-65 b/g; IanDagnall Computing 80-81 c; Trinity Mirror-Mirrorpix 89 cl; PhotoStock-Israel 95 cl; Nature Picture Library 104, 179 bl; Chris Willson 105 tr; Petr Bonek 116-117 b/g; Pictorial Press Ltd 117 tl; Buddy Mays 118 tr; Realy Easy Star 118 bl; travelpixs 121 tr; The History Emporium 121 cl; Westend61 GmbH 122 cl; R-Type 130 bl; Gato Desaparecido 136 bl; Dale O'Dell 137 b; North Wind Picture Archives 138 br; Biosphoto 141 tr; Daniel Eskridge 151 cr; World History Archive 154 t; Genevieve Vallee 164 bl; 165 tr; Cavan Images 185 bl.

Getty: Keystone cover tr, 67 cr; Hulton Archive 7 cl, 100 cr, 100 bl, 117 br; Transcendental Graphics 10 cr, 97 b; LMPC 13 tr; Irfan Khan 19 tr; john finney photography 26 tr; DigitalGlobe-ScapeWare3d 32 cr; gremlin 33 cr, 89 br, 187 tl/ Anadolu 34-35 bg; Chicago History Museum 35 tr; Alex Rodas 35 br; Puripat Wiriyapipat 44 b; louhan 46 tr; duncan1890 47 tr; Glowimages 48-49 b/g; ullstein bild Dtl 51 cr; Planet One Images 54-55 b/g; elleon 57 cr; AFP 58 br; Oxford Scientific 61 br; API 66 br; Mirrorpix 67 bl; AndyRoland 71 tr; Florilegius 75 tr; Best View Stock 77 cr; Cesar Manso 81 bl; Matt Anderson Photography 82 bl; powerofforever 84 cl; Michal Krakowiak 85 cl; Stock Montage 92 c; DEA Picture Library 101; picture alliance 102 br; Thomas Coex 109; VW Pics 110 br; RugliG 111 cl; Cultura RM Exclusive/Albert Lleal Moya 111 bl; Dorling Kindersley 114 b; Eric Meola 120 tl; Florilegius 124, 126-127 b/g; Kevin Schafer 125 tr; SeppFriedhuber 128-129 b/g; derejeb 131 tl; JAXA/Michael Benson 135 bl; Nataniil 141 b; Ankur Khandelwal 144 cl; John Elk III 146 tr, 149 t; imageBroker-Michael Runkel 147 t; Bettmann 155 b; Roman Garcia Mora-Stocktrek Images 161 cr; Fairfax Media Archives 162 cl; Emma Shaw-Lonely Planet 163 bl; CraigRJD 167 cl; atakan 171 bl; takepicsforfun 174-175 b/g.

Other: Adobe Stock IB Studio 6, 27; Roger Patterson and Robert Gimlin 6 br, 18 cl; John Manard 28 c; Walters Art Museum 40 bl; Norris R, Norris J, Lorenz R, Ray J, Jackson B 42 bl; Pedro Szekely 46 cl; Maggie Li 47 cl; The Michael C. Rockefeller Memorial Collection, Metropolitan Museum of Art 49 b; Bernhard Edmaier-Science Photo Library 56 br; Justin Foulkes-Lonely Planet 71 br; Y-Rex 74 cr; Guy Moberly-Lonely Planet 88 tr; NASA 98 br, 99 bl, 169 cl; Morgan710 103 br, 106 b, 120 bl, 130 b/g, 136 tr; iStock ViewApart 110 b/g; JW Hurter 128 br; Shah Rogers Photography 131 cl; Mark Roy 144-145 b/g; Daniel Case 145 tr; Fandorine1959 145 b; Keith Brooks 155 t; Teo Georgiev 160-161 b, 186 bl; Mike Freer-Touchdown-aviation 170 t; Eoin Coveney 181 br; Alasdair Turner- GOLF 4-3-9 Antarctica Expedition 2012 185 t.